St. Louis Community College

Library

5801 Wilson Avenue
St. Louis, Missouri 63110

Guide to Meeting Reading Competency Requirements

Guide to Meeting Reading Competency Requirements:

Effective Diagnosis and Correction of Difficulties

Donald C. Cushenbery

Parker Publishing Company, Inc.
West Nyack, N.Y.

Library of Congress Cataloging in Publication Data
Cushenbery, Donald C.
  Guide to meeting reading competency requirements.

  Bibliography: p.
  Includes index.
  1. Reading—Remedial teaching. 2. Reading
disability. 3. Competency based education.
I. Title.
LB1050.5.C86   428.4′07   81-9524
ISBN 0-13-370353-3   AACR2

Printed in the United States of America

HOW THIS PRACTICAL TOOL CAN HELP YOU

Knowing how to read and function at a literate level in today's world is both necessary and useful if one is to be a productive member of this society. Thousands of young people who have marked reading difficulties are promoted each year to the next grade or learning level. In most states, these persons need to pass state-mandated reading competency tests. In many instances these children could have been helped through an effective program of diagnosis and correction of their reading difficulties, a program which is described in this book.

Early and continuing diagnosis of the learner's problems is a prerequisite to any viable program of correction. The teaching-learning process is not complete unless diagnosis is followed with a step-by-step set of procedures for overcoming reading problems. The medical model demonstrates that the classroom teacher must follow any diagnostic program with a specific list of corrective instructional prescriptions. The central purpose of this book is to guide the classroom teacher in the establishment and use of basic teacher-tested procedures for effective diagnostic and corrective reading instruction at all learning levels. Special emphasis is given with respect to how these procedures can help students develop required competencies in reading.

The emphasis is on the practical, "how-to-do-it," techniques for the teacher who is facing large numbers of pupils with challenging reading problems. I have had long experience in directing reading workshops for experienced classroom teachers and have come to appreciate the precise help that instructors need.

One of the many helpful features of this guide is the

special emphasis given to dozens of easy-to-use techniques which can be used in any classroom where printed materials are used. The techniques are targeted to the *basic* competencies demanded in reading by virtually all state legislatures and school boards. The organization of the volume is designed for easy use by all teachers; however, those junior and senior high teachers who instruct troubled readers will find the material especially straightforward and practical.

STUDENTS MUST PASS READING COMPETENCY TESTS AND TEACHERS CAN HELP THEM ACHIEVE THIS GOAL. THIS INNOVATIVE, UNIQUE, NEW PROFESSIONAL SOURCE AIDS EVERY TEACHER, REGARDLESS OF BACKGROUND, IN PROVIDING DOZENS OF PRACTICAL, CLASSROOM-TESTED TECHNIQUES WHICH ARE AIMED DIRECTLY AT MEETING THE NEEDS OF DEFICIENT READERS.

The organization and length of the volume have been determined with the thought that readers want a source which covers the basic areas and is neither too brief nor too burdensome and complex due to length or sophistication. The decision regarding chapter titles was agreed upon after careful consideration of the essential aspects of diagnosis and remediation as well as analysis of comments and suggestions of beginning and experienced instructors.

Each chapter has at least three features: An organized, well-developed body of specific information; a summary; and a list of suggested references. The material is divided into logical segments which are highlighted by meaningful subtopic headings.

Chapter One directly attacks such important topics as principles of selecting pupils for diagnosis, descriptions of seven extremely useful informal reading tests, and the processes related to other individual and group reading diagnostic techniques.

In Chapter Two, a *classroom* setting is given for a description of such facets as the proper utilization of diagnostic test data, the selection and assignment of teaching materials, and how to construct a total teaching program. Chapters Three, Four, and Five are designed to provide you with many practical, teacher-proven techniques for developing and evaluating the core reading skill areas of vocabulary, word analysis, and comprehension for meeting competency standards. Chapter Six presents interesting and innovative topics concerning home and work related reading assignments. Since state-mandated competency tests *stress* this aspect, you and other teachers and administrators will find this material extremely helpful. To my knowledge, no other current text has this chapter title.

Motivation, one of the most neglected textbook topics, is emphasized in Chapter Seven. This aspect is the *most requested* topic of teachers at the dozens of reading workshops conducted by me. Chapter Eight contains information which is sadly overlooked by the vast majority of the writers on this subject. The practical, direct methods for meeting the individual needs of students in a *group* situation are described.

The appendices of five previous professional books compiled by me have proven to be valuable features according to the many oral and written comments of hundreds of teachers and other educators who have used them. Four important current appendix sections have been included in this volume: selected materials for corrective reading; commercial tests for reading diagnosis; an annotated bibliography of useful professional books for use by the busy classroom teacher; and a list of publishers and addresses.

The ideas and generalizations described in this volume are the products of my thirty-six years' experience in working with hundreds of disabled and retarded readers from ages five to seventy-five. During this time, I have served as a rural teacher, elementary teacher and principal, laboratory school supervisor, university reading clinic director, coordinator of a university graduate reading curriculum, and director of reading workshops involving thousands of teachers in at least thirty states.

To summarize, this book offers the classroom teacher

immediate, practical solutions to the instructional problems of dealing with the needs of students who face competency tests. I have personally used and tested every teaching suggestion included. You can use them right now in *your* teaching program.

Donald C. Cushenbery

ACKNOWLEDGMENTS

The completion of this volume would not have been possible without the help of many persons. I would like to express my special appreciation to Pat Gibson, Ann Fox, Kay Magness, and Barbara Levitan of the Special Education and Teacher Education Departments of the University of Nebraska at Omaha; Kathy Eichhorst, the manuscript typist; Theresa Shepard, the proofreader; all of my students and peers who encouraged me to compile the work; and finally to my wife, Elfrieda, who was patient and understanding during the many months of manuscript preparation.

CONTENTS

3 DEVELOPING VOCABULARY SKILLS FOR READING
COMPETENCY   75

4 CORRECTING WORD ANALYSIS DEFICIENCIES
OF PROBLEM READERS   101

5 BUILDING READING COMPREHENSION
AND STUDY SKILLS   127

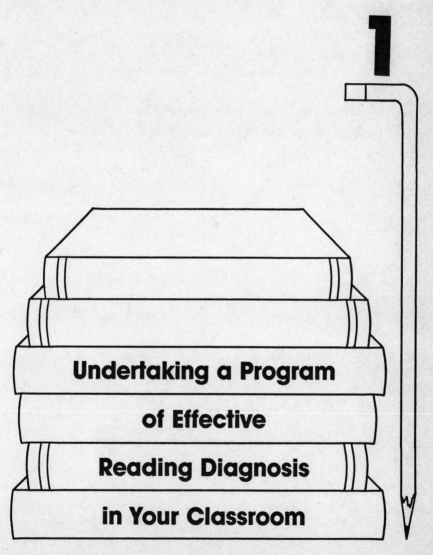

Undertaking a Program

of Effective

Reading Diagnosis

in Your Classroom

One of the most important aspects of any instructional pattern for reading is that of diagnosis. Diagnosis is essential for any type of remedial program because the teacher must know the reading instructional needs of each child. There are a number of factors involved if one is to undertake an effective diagnostic program. It is the purpose of this chapter to describe five different aspects of an effective program of diagnosis.

The *first* major topic discussed is that of the factors associated with reading difficulty; *second*, a discussion of the meaning of diagnosis is conducted; *third*, strategic information is outlined involving how to select pupils for diagnosis; *fourth*, descriptions of seven useful informal reading tests are provided; and *last*, several teacher-tested methods of informal diagnostic techniques are explored. At the close of the chapter, you will find a summary of the information as well as a short bibliography of professional sources for exploring certain topics at greater length.

FACTORS ASSOCIATED WITH READING DIFFICULTIES

At the present time, there are many causes of reading difficulties. Many researchers in the field of reading have come to the general conclusion that there is no one *single* cause of reading deficiency.

It is fair to say that in any given situation a number of factors have contributed to the problems of a particular reader who may have severe reading difficulties at a certain grade level.

We can, however, isolate at least five major causes of reading deficiency and group these under five headings. The first major heading that we can delineate is that of emotional and social problems; the second major category is educational causes; the third, environmental deficiencies; the fourth, intellectual difficulties; and the fifth major cause is physical problems of a given learner. In the following sections, an explanation of the importance of each one of these facets is surveyed.

Emotional and Social Factors

Many of the students who are regularly referred to reading clinics experience various degrees of inadequate personal and social adjustment. Some pupils with significant reading difficulties also exhibit some kind of maladjustment which can be quite severe. The exact relationship between emotional problems and reading problems has not been proven to date. In some instances a severe reading problem may cause an emotional problem, while on other occasions an emotional problem may create a reading problem. When these conditions exist, social problems and inadequate relationships with peers may result.

An aspect of social development is that of language building. A child who has an inadequate oral language may have come from a home where there was not sufficient imitable language on the part of the parents and older brothers and sisters. Typically, this is one of the deficiencies that may be manifested in very disadvantaged children, in bilingual children, or children who have lived in environments where there has not been a rich atmosphere of written or spoken language. At the present time, this aspect of language development may be more important than at any other time in our history because of the influx of children from other countries. These children are at a considerable disadvantage since one of their first tasks is to learn the English language and the meanings for all of the thousands of words. (We must remember, however, that a child's lack of proficiency in English does not indicate lack of intelligence.) Since one of the most difficult tasks a child has is that of learning oral language and identifying the printed symbol that stands for a given word, this aspect assumes considerable importance. Therefore, during the evaluation process, a very careful diagnosis must be made of the child's emotional and social structure if his/her needs are to be met in an adequate manner. Procedures for undertaking this type of diagnosis will be indicated in later chapters.

Educational Causes

According to Wilma Miller,* many cases of reading problems in the elementary school are caused by either inadequate or improper reading instruction, especially in the early primary grades. She further states that many school personnel are not happy to acknowledge this since they believe it reflects unfavorably on them; however, it must be accepted as a fact. Unfortunately, as the older child's reading problems are diagnosed, it becomes apparent that these problems may be the result of a lack of phonics and other skills training at various stages of the child's earlier schooling. These deficiencies in a child's training may have been caused by frequent change of schools or perhaps by a teacher's inadequate training. In other instances, the teachers have not had sufficient experience to meet the needs of problem readers.

In some cases, teachers either have chosen not to retain a child in a given grade or have not been allowed to take this action because of the objections of the parents. This can be unfortunate because in selected cases retention might prove to be useful and valuable.

---

*Wilma Miller, *Identifying and Correcting Reading Difficulties in Children.* (New York: The Center for Applied Research in Education, Inc., 1971), p. 35.

Inadequate provision for meeting individual needs of children has been a problem in many schools. Many children have been forced to read grade level material when, in fact, the particular material was too difficult for their own abilities. In other situations, class size has been too large for a teacher to accommodate all of the instructional needs of the children. Therefore, some children have suffered from lack of attention on the part of the teacher.

In other situations, teachers have not had adequate equipment or materials to meet the needs of the children. The materials have been inappropriate for use with the children in still other schools.

One of the most controversial issues in the past, and indeed at the present, is that of the amount of phonics that has been taught in various grade levels. There are groups of individuals in this country who insist that the reading problems of older children can be traced to a lack of phonic instruction in the lower grade levels. We know about 86 percent of the words of the English language are indeed phonetically regular. This aspect needs to be assessed very carefully. If a teacher is using one of the nationally known basal reading series, he/she is probably providing adequate phonics for most children.

In summary, we need to evaluate all of the aspects of reading difficulties which might be related to educational causes. This is a very important part of diagnosis and should be considered in the most serious light.

Environmental Factors

Consideration of the environment of the child is strategic to the whole process of diagnosis and remediation. Bond, Tinker and Wasson* contend that quarreling parents, broken homes, child neglect, child abuse, overprotection, parental

---

*Guy L. Bond, Miles A. Tinker, and Barbara B. Wasson, *Reading Difficulties: Their Diagnosis and Correction*, 4th ed. (Englewood Cliffs, N.J.: Prentice-Hall, Inc., 1979), p. 101.

domination, anxiety, hostility, and destructive rivalry among siblings are likely to produce nervous tension and feelings of insecurity. Since we know it is imperative that children be extremely secure in the home setting, this factor must be considered. There are many sociological trends in the nation that are most disturbing for teachers and psychologists. It is estimated, for example, that at least one child dies every four hours in this country due to child abuse. The rate of separation of families and attendant difficulties with the family unit have serious implications for the environmental climate of children.

Indeed, for many children, the life they have led is not favorable for learning because they feel unloved and unwanted. In some instances, a child is an object of indifference on the part of the parent and therefore develops an inadequate or poor attitude with regard to schooling in general. In other cases, there is overprotection on the part of parents, while other parents may expect too much of children.

In some instances, there is a vast amount of sibling rivalry in the home. Sometimes parents compare one child with the other. When this takes place, there is a great deal of feeling of insecurity on the part of the child. Accordingly, the child may well develop very unsatisfactory attitudes with respect to reading.

In other situations, a child is in an environment in which he/she sees a parent, brother, or sister who is dying from some terminal illness. This unfortunate circumstance creates feelings of deep distress in the home setting and detracts from the child's attention to the reading act. Therefore, the teacher needs to make a very careful survey of the pupil's home environment. This can be done by asking tactful questions of the child, by receiving information from parents in school conferences, and by checking the child's school record as it seems feasible and legal. Teachers must understand that they are teaching the whole child and not just dealing with reading as an aspect of the child's educational program. You should remember that reading is a *process* and not a formal subject.

Intellectual Difficulties

Many years ago it was thought that children who had not gained a mental age of at least 6.5 could not adequately engage in formal reading activities. At the present time, we have found that, although intelligence has an interesting and positive correlation to reading success at the higher grade levels, it is not nearly as important as we have felt it to be in the past. In many cases, the child with a below normal level of intelligence is able to compensate for the deficiency through a rich background of readiness or eagerness to learn.

There is one reading potential formula that makes the IQ a highly significant item. The one used by many reading teachers is the Bond and Tinker Formula,* which is stated as number of years of school attendance times IQ plus 1. Therefore, if the formula is used directly, it will give some idea of the *estimated* potential of the child. Thus, one would not expect the pupil in the beginning of the fourth grade with an IQ of 80 to be reading at the same level as a child who has an IQ of 130.

One of the most strategic items related to overall intelligence is vocabulary. Therefore, a child deficient in written or spoken vocabulary will probably score at a lower level on an intelligence test. If possible, it is quite desirable to estimate a given learner's intelligence by use of an individual intelligence test rather than a group intelligence test. Group intelligence tests tend to be reading tests and are, in many instances, not as good a sample of the child's behavior as an individual test. Some reading authorities have the opinion that the factor of intelligence may be one of the less important aspects of a pupil's total reading deficiency. This may be true for a number of reasons, among which is the longstanding controversy over whether or not we can measure intelligence, and, indeed, even what intelligence means.

---

*Bond, Tinker, and Wasson, p. 62.

Physical Difficulties and Their Relationship to Reading

According to many learning authorities, the aspect of physiological condition may be the most basic to all human learning and growth. Therefore, if you are to diagnose a learner's reading difficulties in a meaningful manner, you must give your most serious attention to this aspect of the child's life. Reading is highly dependent upon the sense organs. One most certainly needs to see the words in a clear, precise manner and must be able to hear the words as they are spoken.

One of the most common physical problems of children is that of visual difficulties. Inadequate vision, caused by nearsightedness or farsightedness, can create a considerable amount of difficulty for the young learner. A very young child must have adequate near-point vision if he/she is to see the printed words and distinguish one word from another. This can be checked by having the teacher observe the child as he/she reads and see if the learner is having any noticeable problems. Other visual problems may be a lack of fusion and improper muscle development of the eye. Many school officials use the Snellen chart; however, this chart is not suitable in some respects. More adequate instruments would consist of such tools as the *Orthorater* or the *Keystone Visual Survey Telebinocular*.

Problems with the auditory senses can be quite significant for the child. In school systems where there is a great deal of importance given to auditory methods such as in the area of phonics, this aspect can be quite significant.

There are a number of ways of evaluating the child's auditory acuity. One of the most inexpensive ways is that of the watch-tick test, which calls for holding a watch about 3 to 4 feet from the child's ear and slowly withdrawing the watch, writing down the distance at which the child can no longer hear the watch. A more precise method would be the use of the audiometer.

In addition to the physical aspects just described, there are other facets of a child's health that should be considered. These would include glandular disturbances such as those of the endocrine or pituitary glands. Malfunctioning of these glands can cause sluggishness and, in some cases, make the child hyperactive. Many of these functions can be corrected by medication. Children with these deficiencies should be under the care of a physician.

There are other childhood disorders such as asthma and tonsilitis that can create excessive school absences and have a significant impact on the development of reading skills. It would behoove each teacher to make a careful study of each pupil's physical history to determine how these conditions may have an impact on the total reading instructional history of any given learner.

In conclusion, physical difficulties must be measured carefully and accurately to determine their relative importance to the total reading skill development of a child. Many of these aspects can be evaluated by the reading specialist and the school nurse; however, many of them should be under the jurisdiction of the medical specialist.

IMPORTANT ASPECTS OF DIAGNOSIS

There are several aspects of diagnosis that must be kept in mind and are important to all teachers. In the section that follows is a description of at least seven different aspects of diagnosis that should be understood by all instructors. This information includes such aspects as the definition of diagnosis and, more important, the purposes of diagnosis.

1. We must approach diagnosis from a broad definition. Diagnosis certainly consists of more than just the administration of commercial tests. It also involves the important areas of astute teacher and clinic observation of a given child. One must not overlook the importance of informal tests that have been constructed for a particular purpose. When you think of the diagnosis of reading skill development of any given student, think of it as a multi-faceted operation. Unfortunately, there has been a body of public opinion in recent years that has tended to overemphasize accountability of teachers and students as reflected by results of commercial tests. Somehow we must convey the idea to the public the meaning and importance of other types of diagnostic instruments. Above all, each teacher needs to understand that there is no one test so perfect and so absolute that it can diagnose perfectly any and all aspects of reading. Therefore, in thinking about a program of diagnosis, remember to include in your thinking many different types of evaluation instruments.

2. The central purpose of diagnosis is to improve instruction. The major theme of any diagnostic program must be that of devising a structure that will deliver meaningful information to the teacher about a given child. Far too many times, information data from tests have been recorded in a child's permanent file and forgotten. Remember that a significant aspect of analysis of reading skills should be that of being *a part* of an instructional program and not simply *apart* from it. There is some risk in accepting this philosophy since diagnosis may reflect unfavorably upon the instruction a student has received. This should not worry you since you should accept the information for what it is and devise a new strategy that may be more meaningful to the student.

This may involve, for example, your changing a whole set of lesson plans and securing new sets of materials. All kinds of lesson plans should be open for review and revision as the results of diagnostic procedures seem to dictate.

3. One of the most important aspects of diagnosis is that all procedures should be done in a competent and thorough manner. If you are undertaking a program of diagnosis, you should be thoroughly familiar with all aspects of the diagnostic procedures. It is much better to use a few procedures in a very thorough fashion than to use many techniques which may be open to question. It may be very helpful for you to have some other professional observe you in the administration of different types of evaluative instruments and provide a constructive critique.

4. Always think of diagnosis as being continuous as well as periodic. Unfortunately, there have been instances in the past when teachers and principals have designated a given week or day during the school year for the administration of a diagnostic test. Perhaps the test represented the *sole* diagnostic procedure for the year. While once-a-year tests have validity and usefulness to the instructor, one must always think of conducting diagnosis on a *daily* basis as well. The needs of students *do* change from day to day and they need new types of teaching strategies. In fact, one of the most valuable pieces of data that can be collected by the teacher would be his/her observations of the child reading aloud or reading silently. In each and every class during a school day, you may notice that a given child appears to have need for phonics instruction because the pupil is not pronouncing words properly. This information is available to you. If one relies only on once-a-year diagnostic tests, this information would not be available until the end of the year, thus, you would not be able to help the student who needs the additional teaching.

5. In conducting a program of diagnosis, it is imperative that one study and analyze patterns of scores. You should not take a single score or a single piece of information from any *one* given test and presume that *that* score indicates the exact skill development level of the child for that skill. In phonics, for example, one might want to look at the scores from a commercial phonics test, the data from an informal teacher-made test, the reaction of the pupil to his/her seatwork exercises with respect to phonics, and the information secured from hearing the child pronounce words aloud. In other words, teachers need to see if there is a consistent trend of strength or weakness in the total diagnostic program for a given skill. Before making any kind of definitive statement about the child's strengths and weaknesses, be sure to substantiate these feelings with the evidence from patterns of scores and not just individual scores.

6. A good balance of commercial and informal tests should be used in a meaningful diagnostic program. All tests have strengths and limitations. Though many persons both within and without the profession feel commercial tests should be the major types of tests given, I would contend from experience that informal tests also have a very useful place in a viable instructional program. You, the teacher, should feel you have a right, and indeed an obligation, to achieve some kind of balance between published and informal tests as a part of the diagnostic program. There are some aspects of reading that *cannot* be evaluated by commercial tests. The love of reading cannot be evaluated appropriately by any known commercial test. The child's reaction, or feeling, about a given statement may not be appropriately evaluated by a standardized achievement test. By the same token, informal teacher-made tests are not data based; therefore, it would not be possible for you to compare your students with other students across the nation. Standardized tests typically have had standardized groups of children applied in the construction stage and you are able to study comparisons.

In summary, standardized and informal tests have both strengths and limitations. They should be recognized in this light.

7. Be selective in the types of diagnostic data you collect. It is possible in interpreting the total meaning of diagnosis to try to collect too much data about a given child. This type of strategy only clouds the issue and does not serve a meaningful purpose. It is better to collect a selected body of data that will apply to a given skill emphasized than it is to collect a large amount of information that may not be important. In any case, one should use only those diagnostic techniques and instruments that will provide the type of direct and specific information needed. It has been my observation that many school districts administer too many commercial tests. There is some question whether all of these children need to be tested for the aspects that are evaluated by the tests.

In conclusion, the meaning of diagnosis involves a number of aspects. We must think of it in a very broad definition. There must be a central purpose for our diagnosis to improve instruction, and we need to be efficient in those diagnostic techniques that are employed with our students. Teachers need to be selective in the kinds of data collected and used. A good balance of commercial and informal tests for this purpose should be chosen. Evaluation should be continuous as well as periodic. At all times, the instructor should study patterns of scores before making any final decisions about a given child's strengths or limitations.

SELECTING PUPILS FOR DIAGNOSIS

When one considers the fact that in any given school building there may be hundreds of pupils with widely varying strengths and limitations, the process of selecting pupils for diagnosis becomes extremely important. Obviously, it is neither necessary nor important to diagnose every child for every skill being taught. An additional consideration is the fact that there exist over one hundred commercial and informal tests. This creates a problem for you in deciding which tests should be administered to which child. By considering the following principles, all equally important, you can gain a better understanding of the types of pupils to be selected for diagnosis.

1. Establish a critical score for each of the skills you are trying to teach in your class. After having decided this critical score of development, apply diagnostic techniques only to those students who fall below this critical score. Obviously, it is a waste of time to administer diagnostic instruments to pupils already achieving satisfactorily in various skill areas.

2. You should work closely with the supportive staff of the school (such as the resource teacher, the school psychologist, and the special education administrator) in determining the tests to be used. Some individual intelligence tests such as the *Binet* and the *Wechsler Intelligence Scale for Children* must be administered by a fully qualified specialist. In other instances, the number of tests administered to a given grade will need to be considered since the interpretations of tests should be a joint effort between teachers and ancillary personnel.

3. Pupils selected for a certain test should be given some kind of rationale or understanding as to why they have been asked to complete a given test. Even young children have a better motivation with regard to the evaluation task if they understand the need or the reason for the administration. One would be wise to explain that the reason for the test is to help the child improve in his/her reading growth and not something the teacher is going to use for the purposes of making a report card.

4. When pupils are selected for a given test, their parents should receive a communication from school authorities relating to the nature and purpose of the test being given. With the advent of new privacy laws passed by Congress and state legislatures, this precaution is extremely important and necessary. Additionally, parents will have a better understanding of the total testing program and will be much more prone to extend cooperation to the teacher and the school in the total program of diagnosis.

5. Pupils selected for a given test should be those who show some evidence that they can profit from the information gained as a result of the administration. Some teachers have been guilty of administering tests to pupils who are totally unsuited for the instruments. Their observed weaknesses or limitations should lead one to know that they will make a very unacceptable score on the test. It is vital, then, that only these pupils who can profit from the administration of a given test should indeed be selected for it. (You should remember that some courts have ruled that if certain types of tests are to be administered to a bilingual child or any child whose primary language is other than English, the child must be provided with a translation of the material in his or her native language or an interpretation must be supplied.)

In summary, a careful analysis of the five principles just described should be taken into account by every teacher who selects pupils for diagnostic instruments. There should be a close match between the student's needs and the purposes of the test or technique. Above all, the pupil and the parent should understand the rationale for the test and how the results of the instrument will be used. If the right pupils are selected for the right tests, the instructional program for an individual child can be greatly enhanced.

DESCRIPTIONS OF SEVEN USEFUL INFORMAL READING TESTS

As stated earlier, reading evaluation has a number of dimensions. These include the use of commercial tests designed for very specific purposes, the construction and administration of teacher-made informal tests, and the careful observation of the child by the teacher in the reading environment. While each of these aspects is important in the evaluation process, we know that, in many instances, instructors place an undue reliance on the use of data acquired from standardized instruments. Experienced reading teachers know that when informal tests are properly constructed, administered, and interpreted, they can provide very useful information for the construction of individual reading instructional plans for each pupil at either the elementary or high school levels. The use of teacher-made tests, particularly those for diagnostic purposes, would be especially important to all teachers at the junior and senior high levels who have students facing competency tests.

The following seven informal tests have been classroom tested by the author and other highly trained professionals and have proven to be very useful in discovering those exact reading deficiencies which older students may have in the learning environment. Each test explained in this section contains enough description to allow you to use it as it is described for *your* own personal needs in *your* given teaching situation. The difficulty of the test items and the length of each test must be altered to suit the needs of the students in your classroom. Obviously, you would not want to give as many items to a fifth grade student as you would to an eleventh grade student. Therefore, particular attention must be given to the purpose of the test and, as stated earlier, pupils should be selected carefully for these informal tests. These and other tests should not be administered to a child who appears to be quite proficient in certain reading skills. Tests should always provide additional information, not that already known to the teacher. There is no one test, commercial or informal, that can possibly evaluate every reading skill for every child. The seven tests described in the next section are not listed in any particular order of importance; therefore, it is necessary to select those that meet the needs of the students being taught.

1. Individual Sight Word Vocabulary Test

The construction of the test is fairly simple and direct. Let us assume you are an eighth grade teacher of basic core subjects and are anxious to find out the sight word vocabulary levels of your students. Using reading formulae (which will be described later), assess the approximate readability levels of several books with the goal of finding those written at the fifth, sixth, seventh, eighth, ninth, tenth, and eleventh grade levels. Find a representative chapter or section in each of the books.

Beginning with the first word of the chapter, take each *seventh* word thereafter and put it in a column until 50 words have been recorded. You may find, for example, in any given list that you will have the same word two or three times. You may find that some words are fairly easy for that particular grade level. You may discover others that are quite difficult. These words should be placed on a piece of stiff cardboard paper in double-spaced fashion and each student should be asked to read the word list that applies to the grade level you are teaching.

The critical score for each of the word lists should be 90 percent accuracy. If a given student does not achieve 90 percent on the grade level word list, use the word list for the grade level material immediately below the level just administered. Proceed to the grade level where the student achieves a 90 percent score. Conversely, if the student achieves a suitable score on the grade level material, keep going to the next higher levels until the pupil receives a score under the 90 percent critical reading score. You may conclude, then, that the instructional level for the student with respect to sight word vocabulary will be that level where he/she scores 90 percent accuracy. Find books and other instructional materials written at that particular level for use with that student.

If you are using this individual sight word vocabulary test with pupils under the sixth grade, you probably should use only a 30-word list. If you are using this test with students in grades seven through high school, stay with the 50-word list. To insure accuracy with this test, have alternate forms of each of these grade level tests, by using other materials than the one used for constructing the original test.

In addition to using the information for proper grade placement of the students, evaluate the material and utilize it for making decisions about possible phonics problems or structural analysis difficulties the student might have. One should use this information to help build meaningful reading lessons in the future for a particular child. Actually, this type of test is, in many ways, superior to some commercial vocabulary tests because you are evaluating the words that are unique to the teaching materials being employed. The importance of this test cannot be overemphasized. If there are large groups of students and an individual administration of the test is not practical, use it in small groups which seem to be compatible. "Spot-checking" students on different words could be accomplished. The individual administration, obviously, is much preferable to any group application that might be made.

2. The Individual Informal Reading Inventory

The use of an informal reading inventory can be of very practical help in finding a pupil's instructional reading level, efficiency in basic word attack skills, oral reading competency, and reading comprehension abilities on the literal, interpretive, creative, and critical levels. This type of information or data can provide the basis for formulating a rather precise individualized reading program that will upgrade the reading skill development of a student at any grade level. If you are preparing students for competency examinations, this type of inventory is *invaluable*.

The development of the inventory requires the selection of a series of graded materials or content books at various grade levels. Following the example in the previous inventory, one could use the same types of selections as those described in that section. For example, if you teach at the eighth grade level, you could find selections from a book written at the fifth, sixth, seventh, eighth, ninth, tenth, and eleventh grade levels. Select a 100 word passage from each of the levels of books chosen. Ask selected students in an individual setting to read the 100 word passages aloud. Record carefully all of the oral reading errors such as substitutions, omissions, and repetitions. If he/she can demonstrate at least 95 percent accuracy while reading the material aloud, the material may be at his/her instructional reading level.

Another part of the inventory can be employed for measuring the silent reading comprehension of a student being tested. In each book used for oral reading, select a 275 to 300 word passage for the student to read silently. After the student has read the passage silently, compile five different kinds of written comprehension questions for the student to answer. One or two of the questions should be concerned with details. Perhaps one question should deal with the main idea and the other a critical reading skill. Another question might quiz the pupil on a vocabulary word or phrase. Give a certain percentage weight to each question, with all the answers adding up to 100 percent. Under this arrangement, some questions may be worth 15 percent and some 25 percent—others may count for only 10 percent.

If the reader scores at least 75 percent on this phase of the test, the material is probably at grade level for this particular student. In those instances where the oral reading accuracy score is much lower than the silent reading comprehension score, the comprehension score takes precedence due to the fact that comprehension is the end product of the reading act and is the most important skill to be measured. Therefore, the level where the student gets at least 75 percent on silent reading comprehension should be considered the student's instructional reading level.

One of the most significant problems in the teaching and learning situation is the assignment of textbook materials too difficult for the learner to read and understand. If students are to pass state-mandated competency tests, they must be well prepared to deal with comprehension. Therefore, it is urgent that assignments be only those from printed materials that are commensurate with a given student's instructional reading level.

3. The Incomplete Sentences Test

One of the important aspects of the teaching-learning environment is that of the teacher understanding and knowing all the information possible about a given student and his/her background. The assessment of reading interests and how a student feels about different matters are vital data if one is to prepare an adequate reading program for the learner. You may wish to ask each of your students to complete an exercise such as the following. Depending on the age of the students, you may wish to alter the phrases a bit to accommodate the interest and needs of a particular group. Use only 8 to 10 phrases with younger children, and 20 or 25 phrases with secondary students. The following are examples of incomplete sentences that might be used:

1. The most difficult thing about reading is
2. I hope I can
3. I believe I am the best
4. I can do better if
5. My favorite subject is
6. I can read books if

In administering an incomplete sentence test of this type, you should assure the students that you will maintain this information in confidence and it is being used only so that you can better understand their needs. Tell them that all of these statements are considered optional, and if they do not wish to complete certain parts of the sentences, that is their choice.

If a student cannot read the sentences, read them aloud in a very relaxed, private setting and note the responses on the test form. In the individual situation, you may be able to get more meaningful information than would be possible in a group setting.

4. Informal Group Functional Reading Test

If one is to help learners to achieve the competencies needed to pass a school or state mandated achievement and competency test, it is necessary to evaluate their respective skill levels in the area of functional reading. Far too many students have difficulty in finding the different parts of a textbook or other content book and, therefore, can't accomplish the reading task the teacher has assigned. If pupils are to derive maximum comprehension from any type of reading material, they should be able to accomplish day-to-day reading tasks of this type. The purpose of this highly useful informal test is to reveal pertinent information regarding each student's ability to handle this type of reading assignment.

Make a duplicated test and construct questions such as the following over the printed material being employed. At the top of the sheet provide a space for the person's name. Write questions such as the following in a list:

1. On what page would you find information about the crops of Argentina?

2. On what page does Chapter 6 of Part One begin?

3. What are the last names of the authors of this textbook?

4. Look at the picture on page 227. According to this picture, what must the weather be like in Kansas in February?

5. Look at Figure 27 on page 276. According to that figure, how many people lived in Council Bluffs, Iowa, in 1980?

6. According to the index, on what page or pages would you find information about the Kansas-Nebraska Act?

7. On what page does Chapter 7 begin?

8. What is the copyright date of your textbook?

You may shorten or lengthen a test of this kind for your group, depending on the grade level you are teaching. For younger children, perhaps only three or four questions would be necessary. If you're working with high school students, you may want to compile as many as 10 or 12 questions. The wording of the test items should be appropriate for the age and maturity level of the students involved.

Use this kind of test not only for your textbooks, but for assigned library books as well. The information from such a test will reveal how well the students understand the different facets of the books. With this information, design an individualized reading curriculum to meet the needs of particular students.

5. Cloze Technique

A technique often referred to as the "cloze" procedure has been used by hundreds of teachers in the past two or three decades to evaluate vocabulary, word attack, and comprehension skill levels of pupils. The test is easily conducted and scored, and reveals some rather pertinent information to the teacher regarding which teaching strategy should be employed. There are many ways a cloze test can be formulated; however, the following description is one used by the writer over the past 20 years with much success and satisfaction. Find a grade level book and choose a passage of approximately 275 words that will likely interest all students. Duplicate the passage for each child using the following guidelines:

1. Type the first sentence as it appears in the material.
2. Beginning with the second sentence, leave every *fifth* word blank until 50 blanks are in evidence.
3. Ask the students to write the word for each blank that they think is the most logical.
4. Check each learner's paper, allowing credit for each word if it is the same word used by the original author of the material *or* the word is a clear, undisputed synonym of the original word.

If the reader's overall vocabulary and comprehension levels are at grade level, he/she should have a minimum of 38 correct out of the 50 blanks. If a score of 45 or more is obtained, the child should be assigned more difficult material. A score of less than 38 may signal that the material is too difficult. Cloze tests employing higher and lower grade level material may be administered until the most appropriate vocabulary and comprehension levels are found for each pupil.

6. Test for Word Recognition Skills for Upper Grades and Secondary Students

The heart of the reading act is word recognition. Before any type of systematic program of instruction can take place, this aspect must be evaluated. The areas of phonics and structural analysis are major concerns on competency tests. This classroom tested instrument is especially helpful for evaluating *your* students in your class today. The critical score for each of the following tests is 80 percent. Any student scoring below this level on a subtest should receive special remedial instruction in that skill. (Information found in later chapters should be most useful in this regard).

NAME _____ DATE _____

Section I
Context Clues

Choose the best meaning for the underlined word from the choices given below the sentence.

1. The man was *tense*.
    a. dropped down
    b. hanging
    c. nervous
    d. spraying

2. The child *continued* to read.
    a. stopped
    b. laughed
    c. kept going
    d. paused

3. Jean *constructed* a house.
    a. built
    b. started
    c. painted
    d. burned

4. He _cracked_ the pitcher and cup.
   a. broke
   b. counted on
   c. mended
   d. bought

5. It is not _customary_ to walk.
   a. easy
   b. difficult
   c. usual, natural
   d. marginal

6. His _residence_ was on 80th Street.
   a. home
   b. car
   c. office
   d. school

7. He was lost in _meditation_.
   a. writing down his ideas
   b. sound asleep
   c. quiet thought
   d. day-dreaming

8. Shake the cake _vigorously_.
   a. strong, with force
   b. the highest limit
   c. on purpose, intentional
   d. casual

9. He lay _relaxed_ on the ground.
   a. stretched out
   b. stiff
   c. frustrated
   d. folded up, in a heap

10. The truck _roared_ down the street.
    a. without a driver
    b. slowed
    c. moved in a jerking or staggering way
    d. loud noises

Score _____ Percent Correct _____

Section II Structural Analysis

Part One: Syllabication
       Divide the following words into syllables.

1. musically	8. kitchen	15. triceps
2. table	9. fable	16. beeper
3. pillow	10. nation	17. tricycle
4. bypass	11. battered	18. motor
5. nickel	12. cypress	19. calculation
6. mustard	13. biplane	20. navigator
7. madhatter	14. classroom	

Score _____ Percent Correct _____

Part Two: Root words, prefixes, suffixes, and inflected end-
          ings.
          Divide these words into their different parts.

	Prefix	Root Word	Suffix	Inflected Ending
1. bewitching -				
2. disbarred -				
3. unlikely -				
4. predetermined -				
5. misfired -				
6. replanting -				
7. beheaded -				
8. unfaithful -				
9. misplaced -				
10. predict -				

Score _____ Percent Correct _____

Section III Phonetic Analysis

Part One: Applying Vowel Principles
       Pronounce these words and groups of letters.

1. fem	4. jer	7. fo	10. hap
2. ho	5. tir	8. pebe	11. taw
3. mu	6. tes	9. rame	12. cain

| 13. moaf | 15. perl | 17. macter | 19. gopping |
| 14. peas | 16. coy | 18. tusing | 20. guple |

Score _____ Percent Correct _____

Part Two: Phonetic Principles

Here is a list of phonetic principles. Put the number of the principle in front of each list of words.

Phonetic Principle:

1. Open syllable
2. Closed syllable
3. Vowel digraph
4. Final e

5. l and w controller
6. r controller
7. diphthong

____ 1.	crate	quote	fate	mate	late
____ 2.	be	me	so	go	re
____ 3.	mat	mut	nit	dig	met
____ 4.	moat	train	sleet	goat	meet
____ 5.	fir	slur	for	fur	nor
____ 6.	paw	tall	caw	ball	stall
____ 7.	soy	cow	pout	boy	out
____ 8.	grate	trice	twice	cute	mute
____ 9.	free	rain	tree	meet	grain
____ 10.	hit	nut	pit	tat	cut

Score _____ Percent Correct _____

7. Basic Phonics Test for Middle Grade and Older Students

The following test consists of seven basic classroom tested informal tests for evaluating the phonics skills of certain students. Phonics, as we have already explained in this chapter, is a very important part of the total reading program and it is imperative that each teacher evaluate this vital segment.

Each of the following tests should be administered individually, with the words typed on 5 by 8 inch cards and handed to the student to look at while he/she is being administered the test. One can keep the actual test on a clipboard and make notations as the student responds. The critical score for each of these seven subtests is 80 percent; therefore, any student who does not score at least 80 percent on each subtest may need remedial teaching in that specific area.

This particular test segment has been used with hundreds of students in clinics and classrooms and has been found extremely valuable to all teachers. Junior and senior high teachers working with seriously disabled readers who will be facing achievement and competency tests will find this quite helpful. Obviously, this test should not be administered to all students. The test should be administered only to the most severely disabled readers. All of these skills are normally learned by the time a child completes the third grade. Thus, any student who is at the fourth grade *learning level* or above should be able to pass all these tests without any difficulty.

Make a profile sheet for each student taking the test so that when the test has been completed you can determine at a glance which students need help on which items. The profile sheet can be in the form of a grid with the names of the tests at the top of the vertical columns and the names of the learners on the horizontal lines.

I. Long and Short Vowel Sounds

Directions: As I read each word, listen very carefully and tell me if the vowel is long or short.

Example: hit   mate   met

1. plate _____
2. apple _____
3. pet _____
4. meat _____
5. dice _____

6. past _____
7. moat _____
8. shelf _____
9. pit _____
10. rate _____

Total _____

II. Long and Short Vowel Sounds

Directions: Read these nonsense words for me. Say the word by making the vowel long. Read the word with a short vowel sound.

Example: ped   sed

1. brid   2. pred   3. trid
   L _____   L _____   L _____
   S _____   S _____   S _____
4. brot   5. blut
   L _____   L _____
   S _____   S _____   Total _____

III. Open Syllable Vowel Principle

Directions: Study these nonsense syllables. Pronounce them for me.

Example: bo   mi

1. pa _____   5. bu _____   8. ma _____
2. tu _____   6. ne _____   9. ri _____
3. ve _____   7. si _____   10. do _____

(Each syllable must be pronounced with a long vowel sound.)

Total _____

IV. Closed Syllable Principle

Directions: Pronounce these words for me.

Example: pas   rif   bot

1. vab _____   6. tas _____
2. wis _____   7. mob _____
3. des _____   8. jup _____
4. rup _____   9. tis _____
5. dem _____   10. rof _____

Total _____

(Each underlined vowel must be pronounced with a short sound.)

V. Final "E" Principle

Directions: Here are some more nonsense words. Try pronouncing these for me.

Example: tese   mave   tofe

1. p<u>o</u>be _____
2. h<u>a</u>me _____
3. t<u>o</u>te _____
4. b<u>e</u>te _____
5. r<u>a</u>fe _____

6. s<u>u</u>te _____
7. r<u>a</u>me _____
8. n<u>e</u>be _____
9. t<u>o</u>de _____
10. m<u>e</u>te _____

Total _____

(Count responses correct only if vowel is sounded long).

VI. Vowel Digraphs

Directions: Look at these nonsense words and tell me how you think they should be pronounced.

Example: r<u>ea</u>t   p<u>oa</u>t   t<u>ui</u>f

1. r<u>ee</u>s _____
2. t<u>oa</u>b _____
3. p<u>oa</u>b _____
4. p<u>ai</u>p _____
5. r<u>oe</u>d _____

6. t<u>ai</u>p _____
7. t<u>ea</u>d _____
8. t<u>oa</u>g _____
9. s<u>ui</u>f _____
10. b<u>ea</u>m _____

Total _____

(Count response as correct only if first vowel is sounded long and second is silent).

VII. Hard and Soft Sounds of "C" and "G"

Directions: Pronounce these nonsense words.

Example: <u>c</u>ep   <u>g</u>af   <u>g</u>ed

1. <u>g</u>am _____
2. <u>g</u>en _____
3. <u>g</u>an _____
4. <u>g</u>it _____
5. <u>g</u>ols _____

6. <u>c</u>of _____
7. <u>c</u>el _____
8. <u>c</u>ie _____
9. <u>c</u>ol _____
10. <u>c</u>ue _____

Total _____

TEACHER-TESTED METHODS OF
INFORMAL DIAGNOSTIC TECHNIQUES

In addition to the numerous informal tests described in the preceding part of this chapter, there are a number of other teacher-tested methods for diagnosing reading difficulties. In the remainder of this section, several of these techniques are explained. Enough description is given for the reader to enlarge upon each of the suggestions and to use them as the situation permits. Some are more practical than others, depending upon the age group. The words and other material used with each one of the tests should be unique and interesting. Use the actual words, if possible, from classroom instructional materials.

1. If you are working with a group of primary pupils, show them a collection of words on individual flash cards and simply ask them to state the letter with which these words start. This would be an attempt to see if the children understand the letters of the alphabet. Also you might want to give a few more words and ask them to tell you which are on the ends of the words.

2. At the middle grade level, devise a group phonetic analysis test in which you would list a group of words and merely ask the students to mark the vowel long or short, or put a line through letters which are silent. In other instances, a different group of words may be used. Ask the students to underline the consonant cluster, the diphthong, or the schwa sound in the words. With yet another group of words, ask the students to draw a line through all the final letters they see in the words. This same type of test can be used at the secondary level by merely making the words longer and more difficult. You may wish to compile the phonetic spelling of certain words and then ask your secondary students to write the conventional spelling of the words. This will give you some insight into the older students' knowledge of basic phonics skills.

3. You may wish to design a structural analysis inventory in which there is a group of words. Ask the students to underline the base or root word in each of the words. In other instances, the students may be asked to underline the prefix or the suffix. In yet other cases, ask them to divide the compound words into syllables by placing a diagonal line between the syllables.

4. Another teacher-tested method for an informal diagnostic technique would be structuring an inventory in context clue usage at the middle, upper grade, and high school levels. In this case devise an exercise in which the students would be asked to underline the word making the best sense in each of the following sentences. For example, write "Mary watched the blue ＿＿＿＿＿ drive by." Supply three word choices: "car," "tree," and "fence." List about ten sentences and then have three choices for each of the blanks. Depending upon the age and maturity of the student, the sentences can be written at varying levels of difficulty.

5. Another highly useful teacher-tested informal technique is that of constructing an inventory in dictionary usage that can provide much valuable information for a classroom teacher. Again, depending upon the age and maturity levels of the students, compile an exercise in which a number of questions relate to a particular classroom dictionary. An example of such a question would be, "On what page are the two guide words 'created' and 'possibility' located?" Another example would be, "According to the dictionary, what is the sound of 'a' in the word 'lately,' which means 'something in the near past'?" Or you may want to ask such a question as, "According to this dictionary, what is the meaning of 'tableau'?" Yet another question might be, "With respect to this dictionary, what word is a synonym for the word 'masterful'?" Dictionary usage can also be evaluated by listing a group of words, putting the definitions of the words in a mixed fashion, and asking the student to match the words with the correct definitions.

Summary

The factors associated with reading difficulties are discussed at the beginning of this chapter. There is no single cause for reading difficulties. The numerous causes of reading difficulties should be carefully assessed and understood when trying to make a determination as to what has created a student's reading problems. The meaning of diagnosis involves a number of aspects. Diagnosis should be thought of in a very broad sense. In all cases, the data secured should be used to help improve a given student's instructional program. Each teacher should carefully select pupils for diagnosis. Not *all* pupils need *all* tests. The wise instructor will select only those tests that are needed to help evaluate a particular skill. The seven informal reading tests previously described have proven to be very useful for all types of classroom teachers. At the close of the chapter, teacher-tested methods outlined are also valuable additions to any meaningful diagnostic program for students. Give the material in this chapter a try. You won't be disappointed.

REFERENCES

1. Bader, Lois A. *Reading Diagnosis and Remediation in Classroom and Clinic*. New York: Macmillan Publishing Co., Inc., 1980. Ch. 1.

2. Bond, Guy L.; Tinker, Miles A.; and Wasson, Barbara B. *Reading Difficulties: Their Diagnosis and Correction* (Fourth Edition). Englewood Cliffs, N. J.: Prentice-Hall, Inc., 1979.

3. Cheek, Martha C., and Cheek, Earl H. *Diagnostic-Prescriptive Reading Instruction*. Dubuque, Iowa: Wm. C. Brown Company, 1980. Ch. 2.

4. Miller, Wilma. *Identifying and Correcting Reading Difficulties in Children.* New York: The Center for Applied Research in Education, Inc., 1971.

5. Thomas, Ellen L., and Robinson, H. Alan. *Improving Reading in Every Class.* Boston: Allyn and Bacon, Inc., 1977. Ch. 2.

2

Organizing Your Classroom

for Corrective Instruction

to Meet Reading

Competency Requirements

Once you have undertaken the program of diagnosis described in Chapter One, the next important instructional task is assimilating the data and preparing to write prescriptions for those students needing additional help. The major purpose of this chapter is to provide information concerning how you can make the transfer from the testing program to the organization of the classroom for strategic teaching of reading skills.

With this in mind, I have selected the following topics for discussion in this chapter. The first topic is that of how to use the diagnostic test data to design the proper classroom learning environment. In the sections which follow, a pertinent discussion is conducted regarding the common types of reading errors and some teaching strategies that might be used for overcoming these different error patterns. One of the current trends in reading instruction is the use of the computer to provide assistance in corrective reading programs for students who have special problems. The last part of the chapter is designed to help you select and use teaching materials, with an explanation of how the daily teaching program can work for *you*. The program described is one being used by dozens of highly successful teachers across the country. With some slight modifications, you can use it in your own classroom and be extremely successful.

USING DIAGNOSTIC TEST DATA TO DESIGN
THE PROPER CLASSROOM LEARNING ENVIRONMENT

During the course of a school year, the cumulative record test file of any given student may become quite bulky with various kinds of test data relating to a number of items such as percentiles and grade placement scores. If you have requested that a student receive testing from educational specialists, you may find that a number of fairly voluminous reports have been compiled for a child. If you have had limited technical training in the use of such diagnostic test data, the following discussion will serve to lend important help in this area.

Analyzing Test Data

There are *four* major principles to keep in mind when analyzing diagnostic test data to design a classroom learning environment. Probably the *most important* instructional task you will have is conducting an analysis of the various aspects of the diagnostic test in order to pinpoint those exact skill areas where the pupil needs specific instruction. A test or a group of tests should be used as a teaching device and the information gained from such tests should serve as the basis for future instructional objectives. Reading specialists have contended for some time that corrective teaching should be as individualized as possible and highly organized in every teaching-learning situation.

A *second* major consideration with regard to the use of diagnostic test data is reading and interpreting the test administrator's manual for basic information relating to such matters as test data interpretation. If the explanation is not clear and you need further information, ask for clarification from someone who is more familiar with the test. In many instances, this kind of help can come from a guidance counselor, the publisher's representative, or a school psychologist. Since the parents of your students will be eager to know what the information means and how it applies to their child, you, of course, need to be very sure that you understand the interpretation of the test data. In all cases, remember that a diagnostic test is quite different from most achievement tests, since most diagnostic tests are without formal standardization groups and one is merely comparing the child with himself or herself on the given test. The real purpose of the diagnostic test is not to compare children, but rather to reveal to the teacher what strengths or deficiencies a given child would have in a particular classroom setting.

A *third* major consideration is remembering that scores from several different kinds of diagnostic tests should be arranged in some kind of meaningful pattern in order to ascertain a particular learner's reading strengths and limitations. There is no one diagnostic test that is sufficient to meet the needs of all students; therefore, information gained from one test may be substantiated or refuted by yet another test. What one is looking for is a *pattern of scores*. In any case, the final conclusions made must always be based on the commonalities that appear to exist when analyzing the scores from a number of different sources.

A *fourth* major aspect of the use of diagnostic test data is that of including *all* the information that might be available to you, the teacher. Some teachers feel informal test information is not as valuable as standardized test information, and thus they seem to analyze and use only standardized test information. As pointed out in Chapter One, many times the information gained from informal diagnostic tests is as valuable as, if not more valuable than, the data derived from a commercial examination.

Designing A Proper Classroom Learning Environment

Assuming you have followed the four principles previously described, how do you proceed to use test data to design a proper classroom learning environment? First of all, decide what skills are to be emphasized in the given classroom. If, for example, you and your school district officials feel the teaching of phonics and reading for details would be two major reading skill areas, accordingly, you should be sure your diagnostic tests evaluate these two important skills. In any given reading-learning environment, the director of the learning (the teacher) must decide upon the skills to be taught, how they are to be evaluated, and how corrective teaching is to take place. Therefore, after obtaining the list of required skills, use the diagnostic test data to indicate those children who are reading below critical levels for each of the skills. The tests described in the previous chapter are most helpful in undertaking this type of project.

Students in your classroom should be placed in small instructional groups for corrective teaching on the basis of their common reading limitations. In one group you may wish to have children who need basic help in reading for main ideas. In the case of a secondary class, the content teacher may wish to have a small corrective class in helping those students who need further instruction in the use of the dictionary, the library, or specialized source books, such as encyclopedias or the Reader's Guide. Forming groups for corrective teaching is quite useful at all age levels through secondary. Contrary to the belief of some educators and well-meaning parents, students don't seem to mind working in small groups if they feel their own skills are being improved. With respect to any kind of grouping procedure, it is important to remember that students in a particular corrective group should be only those who have designated deficiencies in a given skill. (In any case, it is quite unnecessary to ask all students in a class to complete a certain assignment when there is some question as to whether these students have the same deficiency).

In organizing the classroom learning environment for students having been designated as limited in various reading skills, one must think of materials and the organization of the room. The information provided in the several indices of this book should be quite helpful in suggesting various types of materials that may be available for constructing corrective reading programs. The important principle to remember is that you must select a wide variety of teaching materials on various instructional levels for meeting the individual needs of the students. An innovative corrective reading program should certainly have large amounts of high-interest, low-vocabulary books and other printed materials for use by older students.

In summary, you should analyze diagnostic test data correctly and design a classroom learning environment that is based on the needs of the students. This practice will help immensely in preparing students to meet competency requirements. School authorities should learn as much as possible about the skills generally required on the competency tests and design reading programs to help the students meet these requirements. This is not intended to suggest that teachers should teach for the tests, but rather to point out that this information can be used to help them streamline teaching objectives for a given school year.

COMMON TYPES OF READING DIFFICULTIES

In administering diagnostic tests and establishing the classroom learning programs, it is vital to designate and classify the common types of reading errors that might be unique to the given child. There are hundreds of small reading errors, but, for the purposes of this chapter, the errors that might be noticed in the three major reading skill components are outlined. These are the common errors in the components of word attack, comprehension, and study skills.

Each of these skill areas is listed in the following section, and the kinds of questions that must be answered with regard to the skills have been enumerated. If the answer is "yes" to one or more of the questions for a given student, that information would represent the types of reading difficulties possessed by that particular learner.

I. Word Attack Skills

    1. When the pupil reads orally, does he/she mispronounce, omit, or repeat words?

    2. Is there a pattern of consonant or vowel errors?

3. Does the student make meaningful or meaningless mistakes in pronouncing words?

4. Does it appear that longer words are more difficult for the student than are shorter words?

5. Is there any evidence that the learner is not aware of the common phonic principles that should be learned by the end of the fourth grade?

6. Does the student have basic knowledge with respect to word elements? (suffix, prefix, root word)

7. Does the learner demonstrate that he/she can break the word apart into meaningful segments?

8. To what degree has the pupil learned the sight words that are commensurate with his/her learning level?

9. Is he/she able to use context clues in a given situation, or is the word pronounced in a haphazard manner without this type of help?

10. Is there any evidence that the student makes meaningful use of the dictionary and other such specialized sources when additional help is needed for word pronunciation and meaning?

II. Comprehension

1. Do the pupil's comprehension problems appear to become more complex as he/she encounters longer stories and paragraphs?

2. At what level(s) of comprehension (literal, interpretative, critical, creative) does the learner demonstrate the most difficulty?

3. Are the basic comprehension difficulties centered around reading for details and main ideas more than in the area of creative comprehension, which asks the reader to make some kind of conscious decision that will affect him/her?

4. Are the comprehension errors more common in oral reading or in silent reading materials?

5. In what content area(s) does the student appear to have the most comprehension difficulties?

6. Do you get the impression that the student understands the types of comprehension errors being made, and is there any defined effort on the part of the student to work with you in overcoming errors?

III. Study Skills

1. Is there any evidence that a given learner is employing the techniques of one of the more noted reading-study formulae, such as the SQ3R developed by Robinson?

2. Does the student have the facility for adjusting reading speed to the difficulty of the material being read?

3. Are the various parts of the textbook fully understood by the student? (subtopics, chapter summaries, reference section, glossary, index, table of contents, etc.)

4. Is there any evidence of lip or head movements while reading silently?

5. Do certain students appear to have a great deal of difficulty in studying material for a unit test?

6. Do some students have difficulty in understanding *how to take a test?* (Readers must have a grasp of this skill; otherwise, they may exhibit a considerable amount of difficulty on district and state mandated competency tests.)

Apply the list of questions above to every student in your classroom. Some of the answers to the questions above can be answered through oral tests and observation, while others will need to be assessed by using commercial diagnostic reading tests of various kinds. If you use a pencil and paper test, be sure that the various aspects of the test evaluate the questions that you have in mind. In any case, your careful observation of a given reader in a particular situation may well be the most important source of information for answering all of these questions.

The degree to which you will be able to help a student overcome his/her difficulties will be dependent upon several factors, including those of the reader's potential for learning, his/her own desire to improve, and the amount of time you may have available for helping the student with these particular difficulties. The important aspect to remember is that the common reading error patterns have been designated for each individual learner, and one or more professionals in the school environment are in the process of undertaking a program to help eliminate these difficulties.

TEACHING STRATEGIES
FOR OVERCOMING PATTERNS OF ERRORS

In light of the fact that the previous section divided the reading error segments into word attack, comprehension, and study skills, the teaching strategies for overcoming deficiencies in these areas will be listed by those same areas in this section. Keep in mind that these are merely representative strategies and by no means are they a complete list of all the different teaching approaches you can use for these given deficiencies. In addition to the various commercial materials described in the following sections, many more suggestions with regard to these kinds of aids can be found in the various appendices of this text. Each of the strategies described must be altered or modified slightly depending upon the age and learning levels of the students for which they are intended. You will need to experiment to observe which of the strategies seem to achieve the best results with a given student. *Detailed* lesson plans for aiding the student in such important areas as vocabulary, word analysis, comprehension, and work related reading assignments can be found in later chapters.

I. Teaching Strategies for Overcoming Word Attack Errors

1. With respect to phonic difficulties, one should always approach the teaching from the analytic rather than the synthetic standpoint. Most reading authorities believe the phonetic analysis is the best approach to use since the study of a word is from the Gestalt or whole-word approach. Accordingly, the various sounds of the words are not distorted and the child is working with larger units in the word; therefore, he/she will not be confused by the innumerable smaller sounds within a given word or series of words. Most basal reading approaches endorse and use the analytic approach. In other words, we are trying to get the child to see the whole word and blend all of the sounds together, rather than trying to say each and every minute sound within a given word.

2. Always use the inductive approach to the teaching of phonics rather than the deductive approach. When using the inductive approach, you should first choose a phonic principle that you would like the children to master, and then choose four to eight words that will illustrate this generalization in a very clear fashion. Ask the children to observe the words and tell you what they think the generalization is. For example, you could write the words "met," "set," "sat," in a list, with the idea that the students would arrive at the logical conclusion that a vowel in a medial position would generally have the short sound.

3. If the student is having difficulties in auditory discrimination, you may wish to use some of the commercial tapes that are being sold to help the child with this important skill. Many of these tapes are included in the description of materials in Appendix A.

4. There are also special commercial workbooks that can be employed to help a child overcome a pattern of errors in phonics. These are useful not only for elementary students, but for high school students as well. The names of several of these suggested workbooks and worktexts can be found in Appendix A.

5. There are also several commercial game kits that have been constructed and marketed in the past several years. Many of these have been quite helpful to teachers in helping children overcome patterns of errors in phonics and other word attack areas. These would include *The Phonics We Use* learning-games kit available from Rand-McNally; *Vowel Lotto* available from Garrard Press; and *Consonant Lotto,* also available from Garrard Press. The addresses for these companies can be found in Appendix D of this text.

6. For those students having difficulty in the area of structural analysis, one may wish to institute some basic lessons in breaking words apart into the various word elements. For example, direct lessons may need to be constructed which would help the student to see the prefix, suffix, and root word in the word "unfaithful"; to see that "un" is the prefix, "faith" is the root word, and "ful" is the suffix. To test the student's knowledge of word parts, you could then have a number of words with various elements present on flash cards, and ask the students to tell what the various word parts would be. Another alternative would be taking long words and cutting them into pieces, putting them in scrambled fashion on top of the table, and asking the student to put the pieces together so they finish with a true word.

7. The Fernald approach can also be used for teaching syllabication. Information about this method can be found in a volume by Rupley and Blair.* This particular method emphasizes several important points, among which are the pronunciation of a word, tracing the word, then writing the word into syllables and blending the syllables together to form meaningful words.

8. There are also a number of commercially available games to teach various structural analysis skills. These are

---

*William H. Rupley and Timothy R. Blair, *Reading Diagnosis and Remediation* (Chicago: Rand McNally College Publishing Company, 1979), pp. 394-5.

described in Appendix A. One of the most helpful commercial aids is that of the *Reading Spectrum* produced by the Macmillan Company. The Garrard Publishing Company also produces various structural analysis games, including *The Syllable Game*.

9. There are a number of ways to help a student overcome sight word error patterns. The exact teaching strategy to be used would be based on the results of the informal and commercial tests which have been administered. One of the simplest and yet one of the most effective methods is simply bombarding the child with flash cards on which the sight words have been printed. For middle, upper grade, and high school students, the use of a commercial tachistoscope may be most appropriate. One of the most famous of the tachistoscopes is sold by McGraw-Hill Book Company and has a number of lessons available for helping a student recognize words by sight in a rapid-fire fashion. A homemade tachistoscope can be constructed by using the instrument found in the *Durrell Analysis of Reading Difficulty* test envelope.

10. One of the most effective methods of correcting problems with context clues is simply providing each student with a series of sentences and with a blank for one of the significant words in the sentence. At the close of the sentence, leave three word choices and ask the student to select the most logical word to go in that blank. In choosing the three words, one word, of course, should be the answer; another word would be one that might possibly be the answer but is not nearly as good as the word just removed; and the third word could be a word that, in the context, is a nonsense word. One could also have a group of students, particularly older students at the high school level, construct context clue exercises, exchange them with each other, and see if their peers can complete the exercises that they have compiled. More detailed information relating to building context clues will be found in the next chapter.

II. Teaching Strategies for Overcoming Patterns of Errors in Comprehension

1. Be sure all the exercises used with students are written at their instructional reading level (i.e., that level where the student can pronounce at least 95% of the words orally and comprehend at least 75% of the information when reading silently).

2. For each and every teaching strategy in comprehension, remember to construct any and all exercises on the basis of the exact reading deficiencies of the pupils in each of the respective areas. For example, if the student is particularly deficient in literal comprehension skills such as remembering important details or drawing together a main idea, one may wish to underline the various key words and phrases of a story and duplicate it for the students to read. This type of strategy will help the students to grasp and to look for these important elements in the future readings that they do.

3. In order to develop the concept of the four levels of comprehension (literal, interpretative, critical, and creative), print a short selection and then pose four questions following it which would illustrate the four different levels of comprehension. This could be done on a transparency with the use of an overhead projector. By using the grease pencil, you could underline the words emphasizing details or a sentence that appears to be the main idea. Point out a sentence that may or may not be true and ask the students, "Now that you've read this story, how is it going to affect your life?"

4. There are a number of commercial materials available for building comprehension and a list of these materials can be found in Appendix A. Two of the most respected materials in comprehension are the *Reading Comprehension Mastery Kits* by Cushenbery and Meyer, published by the Center for Applied Research in Education; and the *Be A Better Reader Series* by Nila Banton Smith, published by Prentice-Hall. Addresses for these companies can be found in the appendices.

III. Strategies for Overcoming Errors in the Area of Study Skills

1. After introducing your students to a number of specialized resource books that they should use for their work in your class, give them a task sheet containing several questions relating to the material in a given source. For example, with respect to the *World Almanac*, you may ask such questions as, "What was the population of New York in 1980?" or "What is the land area of the state of Wyoming?" After conducting such an exercise, be sure you have future lessons which call for this skill to be used.

2. An alternative to Number 1 would be simply listing a number of study skill questions on a sheet of paper. On the right side of the paper list specialized sources, and ask the students to select the resource book that probably would be most helpful in finding the requested information for each item.

3. In helping the students adjust reading speed, one may wish to list several questions on the greenboard or the transparency which would call for varying reading speed levels. Point out that a good reader is one who reads at varying levels, depending upon the task at hand. Ask such a question as, "Would you read at a very slow or a very fast rate if you wanted to know the name of the title of Chapter IX?" "How would you read if you wanted to find the name of the five major crops of Argentina as they are described in Chapter IV?" If students have difficulty with this type of exercise, proceed to further corrective lessons in pointing out the names of the subtopics, the given book, italicized words, and chapter summaries. All of these strategies will help *your* students tremendously in preparing themselves for meeting reading-competency tests used in many states (in fact, the major emphasis of this book is for this purpose, and each and every suggestion listed has been classroom tested and designed to meet this particular need).

COMPUTER-ASSISTED INSTRUCTION
IN CORRECTIVE READING PROGRAMS

There are several electronics companies that are manufacturing and selling computers to schools for use with students in various learning situations. These computers range from fairly inexpensive models to some that involve several thousand dollars. All of this equipment is reasonably simple to operate and provides the student with immediate feedback and responses to different kinds of learning problems and situations. School officials can make their own programs for the computer based on the curriculum unique to that school system. Commercial programs are also available that deal with nearly all of the reading skills described earlier in this volume.

One of the major advantages of computer-assisted instruction is the fact that these instruments provide many more teaching strategies for a given teacher than could possibly be available through software printed materials. When several data banks are connected into a common unit, a given student may literally have dozens of teaching plans available to him/her. Some of the computer programs are available only through commercial outlets, while others are sold directly to schools for use by teachers. One of the major commercial programs is that of the Plato Learning System marketed by Control Data. Two of the more common commercial computers available to schools for corrective reading instruction are the Apple programs sold and distributed by Computerland; and the TRS 80 Model 1, which is sold by Radio Shack stores across the country. The major difference between Plato and the Apple and TRS programs is the fact that the data bank for Plato is in one central location in the United States, whereas the Apple and the TRS 80 depend on specially prepared discs that are either commercial or teacher-made.

If finances permit, the use of computers for corrective instruction in reading is recommended. As more mass production takes place, no doubt the cost will be reduced and the instruments will be more widely available to schools. It is not thought that computers will ever take the place of a classroom teacher, but they can provide important assistance to students in overcoming reading difficulties. The names and addresses for Control Data, Computerland, and Radio Shack are all included in the appendices of this volume. You can also consult the Yellow Pages of your phone book for the store in your area that markets these and similar computers.

SELECTING AND UTILIZING TEACHING MATERIALS

One of the dilemmas most teachers and administrators encounter is that of selecting and purchasing appropriate materials to help their students overcome a reading difficulty. One needs only to visit the book exhibit area of a national convention, such as the International Reading Association, to understand that there are over one hundred companies presently publishing, distributing, and selling both hardware and software materials to schools for corrective reading instruction.

Since most schools operate on a very limited budget, the matter of what principles to apply in the selection and utilization of teaching materials becomes very important. Accordingly, one should keep in mind the following principles in making these important decisions:

1. Small amounts of desired materials should be purchased for the purpose of field-testing these materials with a representative sample of students in your district. The practice of testing the worth of a given set of materials in a pilot project is always a good policy before any large purchases are made. This is very important because, in some instances, publishers may have field-tested their materials with students who are not typical of the type of students common to your school. At the conclusion of the pilot project, there

should be an assessment of the value of the materials made by corrective reading teachers and classroom teachers. Evaluations from students should also be utilized. Many times teachers fail to recognize the importance of information that they can secure from students. After all, it is the students who will be using the teaching aids.

2. All materials, both hardware and software, purchased and used in a given educational setting should always correlate very closely with the reading objectives being pursued by a teacher. Many times materials are made for general use of the teaching profession without regard to the individual needs of teachers. You should, in analyzing the materials, assess the types of exercises which are supplied, and make a determination as to whether or not these exercises do in fact help the students with their instructional problems. In this regard, it may be very important for you to use readability formulae to determine if the readability levels of the materials coincide with the reading instructional levels of the students who will be using them.

3. The teaching aids purchased should be of the type which are self-corrective in nature and provide the student with immediate feedback. One should pay particular attention to the types of instructions that have been provided by the publisher to decide whether or not these guides provide ample direction for the proper use of the aids. If materials demand a heavy allocation of time on the part of the teacher, you may decide to give a less favorable rating to this type of material. This would be particularly true if you have a large number of students in a corrective situation. Above all, remember that there is no one set of materials that can possibly meet all the needs of all your students. If corrective reading instruction is to take place in a meaningful manner, many different

types of materials will need to be purchased for meeting the individual needs of the students

4. All of the materials purchased should be of the kind that would allow the various components to be assigned to students in an individual setting. The materials should be arranged in some kind of meaningful fashion so the student can find them easily during the period assigned to corrective reading instruction. If your school has a special resource materials room, place all of the materials dealing with word attack in one section of the room, others associated with comprehension in another part, and materials emphasizing resource teaching and study skills in yet another section of the room.

5. Materials purchased for use in a corrective reading program should be those that allow the student to develop a sense of success in the daily teaching-learning environment. This is an old saying, "Nothing breeds success like success" and this is certainly true about the materials that you purchase and use. Accordingly, it would be desirable to see if the materials have some kind of progress charting that would help the student to understand the amount and degree of success he/she might be having with that particular material. This would also be of benefit to the teacher in determining whether or not the material is appropriate for the student to whom it has been assigned.

6. One must not overlook the value of teacher-made informal materials that might be constructed and used for corrective reading lessons. For example, a committee may desire to build a reading skills box. The following is a description of how to make the box.

Materials Needed:

4 or 5 copies of workbook or other material to be used (2 pupils' copies, 1 teacher's copy)

9″ × 12″ tag board
⅜″ masking tape
colored tape—miscellaneous colors.

Procedure:

1. Cut the workbook so that all pages are separate.
2. Tape all exercises to a piece of stiff cardboard with even-numbered pages showing. Repeat the process with all exercises on odd-numbered pages. Sheets may be laminated for durability.
3. Choose a different color of tape to represent each skill area. Place the tape on the top (back and front) of each exercise sheet. The tape should be on the upper left hand corner of the card. The skill lessons can be easily found with this process.

   A suggested color key is as follows:

   orange - single consonants
   brown - consonant blends and speech consonants
   yellow - short vowels
   red - long vowels
   blue - vowel groups
   green - structural analysis exercises

4. Choose a circle of a different color to represent each grade level. Place the circle on the upper right hand corner of the card.

   Colors that may be used are as follows:

Grade	Color
1	blue
2	yellow
3	green
4	orange
5	red
6	black
Jr. High	brown
Sr. High	purple

If kits are exchanged among classrooms, the same colors should be used in all boxes. Information regarding the meaning of colors or grade level designations should not be revealed to students.

5. The individual cards are now ready to be put into a container. They should be set on edge so that the colored tape markers show. Make a cardboard divider with the circle indicating grade level to separate each workbook from the others.

If each teacher in a given building would have this type of box and exchange it with other teachers in the same school, the total faculty would have access to literally hundreds of different types of lessons for corrective reading.

It is important to remember that materials don't teach students. Teachers do. There is no positive correlation between the amount and cost of materials and the degree of success that students realize in any given reading program. The most important ingredient in any reading program is the competency of the teacher. The types and kinds of materials are of secondary importance. A good teacher who has a number of carefully selected materials will be in an ideal environment for maximum development of reading skills on the part of students who have various designated deficiencies.

THE DAILY TEACHING PROGRAM AND HOW IT CAN WORK FOR YOU

Since it has been established that the teacher is the *most* important element of any corrective reading program, the importance of the careful construction of daily teaching programs cannot be overemphasized. If the daily teaching program is to succeed, there are at least four important steps that must be followed by an innovative teacher at any particular level. These steps are absolutely critical to those of you preparing your students for state or local competency examinations.

The first step in preparing a meaningful daily teaching program is to decide what skills you want your students to master. The skills that you designate in this step may be the skills you personally emphasize or those emphasized by the reading program that has been adopted for your school system. More important for secondary teachers, the elements stressed on mandated competency tests may be a paramount consideration. Again, this is not to say that we should teach for the tests, but rather that we should sharpen our focus on the skills that should receive major importance in our teaching program. The list of skill competencies may be short or long term. This determination will, of course, need to be made by you and other individual teachers. *In the case of competency examinations that are administered during the senior year, all teachers who use printed materials with students will need to think of corrective reading instruction on a long-term basis.* Short-term skill goals should be designed for daily and weekly lesson plans.

The second step in a daily teaching program would be that of evaluation. After you have determined the skills you think are important and appropriate for your students, you need to apply various diagnostic techniques to decide whether or not your students possess these skills. For example, if you have determined that the students in your room need to be proficient in interpretative comprehension skills, provide sample lessons that will test whether or not the students can claim this competency. Many states that have competency examinations provide sample questions for use by schools. These might be cues as to the types of skills you should evaluate.

The third major step in your daily teaching program would be that of writing prescriptions and making assignments on an individualized basis for those students who need to improve certain reading skills. This would necessitate your understanding all the printed and non-printed materials that may be available within and without your room for the kinds of lessons that you design. After students have had a chance to complete the assignments you have given, then it is time to go to the next step.

The fourth major step in the daily teaching program is evaluating to see whether or not your teaching assignments have helped the student develop desirable reading skills. Even though your intentions were based on rather scientific knowledge of what you felt a given student needed, you may discover the assignment you had him/her complete did not achieve the goal you had in mind. If this is the case, you will have to restructure your assignments to better meet the needs of the students. It may demand that you select different reading materials, or it may call for you to work with students in an individualized rather than a group setting.

With regard to the daily corrective teaching program, it is important to remember that all teachers who use any type of printed material are, in fact, reading teachers. All junior and senior high teachers reading this volume should understand that *whatever* content area you teach, you certainly will be involved with students in building word attack, vocabulary, and comprehension competencies. The vocabulary and other skills unique to your content area must be developed by *you. There is no one reading specialist in any one building who can possibly take care of all the reading needs of all the students. Development of reading competencies for older students—in fact for all students—is a job of the total faculty.* It is not the job of any one teacher, such as the reading teacher or the English teacher. If you have not had adequate training in the teaching of reading, this volume has been *especially* designed to help you in your important task as a corrective reading teacher. The suggestions included have been extensively tested and found to be practical and useful by literally hundreds of teachers just like yourself. Give them a try in your class beginning *today*.

Summary

In this chapter, several important topics have been discussed that are designed to help you organize your classroom for corrective instruction to meet competency requirements. You should use diagnostic test data to design a proper classroom learning environment in the manner that has just been described. There are several common types of reading difficulties and each student should be assessed to discover which of these types he/she might possess. There are a number of proven teaching strategies available to teachers for overcoming these types of errors. There are also computer-assisted programs available to teachers and, where finances and school policy permit, a careful investigation of the value of these instruments should be undertaken. These computers can be of much help to the busy teacher. Since there are hundreds of companies producing materials for teachers, it is important that you select and use teaching materials in the most careful manner, as described in this chapter. There are four important steps to the daily teaching program: (1) determination of skills to be mastered; (2) evaluation of students to determine the competency of each student with respect to each skill; (3) assignment of prescriptions to each student based on their respective needs; and (4) further evaluation to see whether or not the teaching strategies have been successful.

REFERENCES

1. Cushenbery, Donald C. *Reading Improvement Through Diagnosis, Remediation and Individualized Instruction*. West Nyack, New York: Parker Publishing Co., 1977. Ch. 9.

2. Fry, Edward. *Elementary Reading Instruction*. New York: McGraw-Hill Book Company, 1977. Ch. 12.

3. Hill, Walter R. *Secondary School Reading*. Boston: Allyn and Bacon, Inc., 1979. Ch. 13.

4. Quandt, Ivan J. *Teaching Reading: A Human Pro-*

cess. Chicago: Rand McNally College Publishing Company, 1977. Ch. 14.

5. Rupley, William H., and Blair, Timothy R. *Reading Diagnosis and Remediation*. Chicago: Rand McNally College Publishing Company, 1979.

6. Spache, George D. *Diagnosing and Correcting Reading Disabilities*. Boston: Allyn and Bacon, Inc., 1976. Ch. 10.

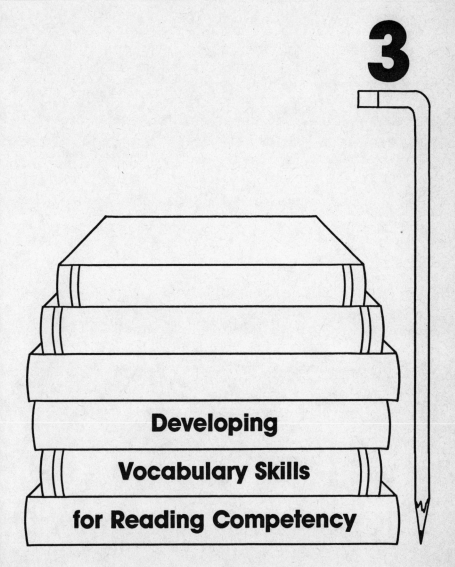

3

Developing

Vocabulary Skills

for Reading Competency

The contribution of different types of vocabularies to the total communicative process cannot be accurately estimated; however, there is a great deal of evidence to suggest that a wide and varied vocabulary is absolutely essential to silent reading comprehension skills and written communication assignments. Vocabulary enlargement must be made a part of every body of objectives and competencies constructed for the language arts curriculum of each school. By reading words and reflecting on their meanings, the pupil gains a vast amount of understanding relative to new words and concepts that he/she may encounter in school reading assignments.

Since one of the leading reading deficiencies of many disabled readers is that of a limited vocabulary, a careful diagnosis must be made of each learner's capabilities in this area. Following the completion of an effective, far-reaching diagnostic program, a prescription teaching and remediation plan should be constructed for pupils at both the elementary and secondary levels in developmental as well as corrective lesson settings.

Developing such strategies in an effective, useful, and meaningful manner requires teachers to have certain skills and information regarding such matters as the nature of vocabulary, the diagnosis of vocabulary, and the teaching strategies necessary to help students enlarge their various vocabularies. The purpose of this chapter is to provide sufficient, practical information for the instructor to help students gain these competencies.

In light of this goal, the following topics are explored: definition of different types of vocabulary, place of vocabulary in the reading process, principles for teaching vocabulary, teaching strategies for correcting vocabulary deficiencies, and evaluation of vocabulary skill development. A summary of the total body of information is furnished at the close of the chapter.

DEFINITION OF DIFFERENT TYPES OF VOCABULARY

The accomplished reader possesses five rather distinct vocabularies. These types have various characteristics that should be considered carefully: vocabulary is enlarged to the degree that there is a great amount of interaction between the reader and the world around him/her; vocabularies grow at different rates; and general vocabulary is positively related to overall general intelligence. There are five general types or kinds of vocabularies that can be identified in the teaching-learning process: listening, speaking, reading, writing, and potential vocabulary.

Listening Vocabulary

Every learner starts the process of vocabulary development by listening to words spoken by parents and playmates and associating these words with objects and concepts with which they are familiar. The degree to which this type of vocabulary is constructed will be highly dependent upon the amount of oral language stimulation the child receives. A young boy or girl living in a very deprived environment where there is little conversation will, of course, have a somewhat restricted level of listening vocabulary.

After a child has had many experiences in listening to words from numerous sources, he/she begins to understand the importance of auditory discrimination. The young person knows, for example, that several words may have the same meaning as in the case of the expressions, "give me your cat," and "give me your kitty." Obviously the alert learner soon realizes that the words "cat" and "kitty" both mean the furry, four-legged pet that lives in the home. The basis for extensive speaking vocabulary is that of the formation of many activities for building a large listening vocabulary.

Teachers can do much to help parents build the listening vocabulary levels of their children. Some of these suggestions might include the following:

1. Engage in daily conversations with children in different life situations in order for them to understand that there are some words with singular meanings and others with plural meanings.

2. Read interesting and varied books and stories to children in a calm, unthreatened atmosphere in order that they might develop a desire to listen for new, unlearned words.

3. Develop listening skills by demonstrating different items that make various kinds of sounds. Several of the better toy and educational materials stores stock toys that emit sounds to imitate different types of animals. These tools lend much support to the building of listening vocabulary.

Speaking Vocabulary

As indicated earlier, the young pupil's speaking vocabulary is correlated highly with listening vocabulary skill levels due to the fact that the first words spoken are merely the imitation of sounds made by parents and siblings. The language code employed by older children and parents will affect the later code developed by the child just starting to build a speaking vocabulary. Those in the home who use long sentences involving a number of descriptive phrases and modifiers in rather complex forms will help the child to build a sophisticated oral language pattern. Experienced primary teachers can soon detect those children who have extensive speaking vocabularies by recording the conversations and oral reports of the pupils during many natural situations as the school day progresses. Those pupils who consistently speak in very short, direct sentences apparently possess very limited speaking vocabularies.

The speaking vocabulary level of the average first grade child has been variously reported in literature as being anywhere from 2,000 to 4,000 words with the listening vocabulary being in the range from 5,000 to 12,000 words. The pupils possessing extensive listening vocabularies, and who are provided with many opportunities to speak, may well develop a documented speaking vocabulary of as many as 6,000 words or more. If this is the case, the child will have an excellent foundation for building and enlarging his/her reading vocabulary.

Success in the establishment of reading vocabulary will be governed by the amount and degree of listening and speaking vocabularies built by the listener. The speaking vocabulary of the pupil continues to increase at the upper grade and secondary levels and may reach as many as 15,000 words or more. For our extensive speaking vocabularies, we are indebted to friends, teachers, and parents. Through the use of imitation and daily involvement by way of intensive oral language, a young learner can increase his/her reading vocabulary in a considerable manner.

The diagnosis and adequate correction of each learner's speaking vocabulary is an important consideration in the teaching-learning model. Those who have demonstrated deficiency levels will need intensive teaching and language stimulation exercises of the type described later in this chapter. These corrective lessons must be conducted on an individual basis due to the fact that each pupil will have needs that vary widely from every other child's.

Reading Vocabulary

The reading vocabulary of most students is not learned prior to entering school unless they have learned to read words taught by a parent or preschool teacher. At the initiation of most formal reading experiences, a sizable list of sight words is taught to children to provide them with early success in the act of reading. In order for them to continue the building of reading vocabulary and general decoding skills, they need to establish a body of competencies in such important areas as phonetic analysis, structural analysis, context clues, and use of the dictionary.

Depending upon a student's overall reading ability, he or she probably will have a larger reading vocabulary than is the case with speaking vocabulary. In the situation of a few seriously disabled readers, the reverse may be true. The assessment of total reading vocabulary is relatively uncomplicated since various informal reading inventories can be used with a miscue analysis applied to the oral reading section. The careful analysis of these data will be of much help to the teacher in determining the frustration, instructional, and independent reading levels.

Writing Vocabulary

The ability to write words that have been heard or read is an important expressive aspect of total language arts. Since the average learner can read and understand more words than he/she can write, the number of words in the writing vocabulary is much smaller than the amount to be found in the other four vocabulary types. An analysis of representative samples of writing will lend important data relative to the type, number, and kinds of words common to any one child's writing vocabulary.

Total writing vocabulary may be enhanced considerably by asking pupils to complete different creative writing assignments that are within their needs and range of interest. An example of such an assignment would be that of supplying the *last* sentence of a proposed story and asking pupils to create a suitable essay that could logically precede the sentence. One might use the following for such a purpose: "And that is why my bathtub was filled with green Jello." Various kinds of writing assignments should be arranged to give pupils a chance to use and reinforce words that have recently been acquired as a part of the reading vocabulary.

Potential Vocabulary

This vocabulary relates to all of the words that any person could understand when many different situations may be present. By using the numerous prefixes, suffixes, root words, and context clues in a given sentence, one might be able to grasp the meaning of many words presently unknown. There is no one figure that can be assigned to this level of vocabulary for any single person, since it would not be known how many or what kind of semantic clues would be needed to comprehend a given word.

At the present time, there are many stimulating mechanisms that have tended to accelerate the level of potential vocabulary for many young people. Television programs containing verbally loaded materials have introduced students to thousands of words previously unknown to them. Creative advertising agencies using various electronic and print media have introduced many new words and concepts to the reading public. Additionally, many up-to-date dictionaries have recently been sold containing new and previously unpublished words. Although there is no accurate definition of the total number of words in an average person's vocabulary, some persons suggest that some first graders may understand approximately 25,000 words; and a twelfth grade student may have access to as many as 85,000 words.

VOCABULARY IN THE READING PROCESS

There is a substantial positive relationship between meaning vocabulary levels and effective literal and interpretative comprehension at both the elementary and secondary levels in all the major content areas. Words of both a general and specialized nature can be found in every school subject. Since comprehension is the end product of the reading process, all students must have a good understanding of word meanings. There is also an interesting and rather significant relationship between vocabulary development and general intelligence. Some educators have the opinion that vocabulary development is a good indicator of overall intelligence since many of the same factors are involved in both areas.

Word recognition or word attack is the heart of the reading process; therefore, a student having knowledge of a sizeable number of sight words is at an important advantage. Phonic skill competencies should be a valuable aid to any reader in the unlocking of unknown words.

If the reading process for a given pupil is enhanced through the use of extensive studies in semantics, the learner will be able to add hundreds of words to his/her meaning vocabulary levels. These activities could be similar to an exercise such as the following involving the use of the word "man."

1. He was a very popular *man*.
2. We will ask each person to *man* a booth at the carnival.
3. The football team lost the game because they were out-*manned*.
4. The boxer *man*handled his opponent and won the match.
5. The basketball team used a *man*-to-*man* defense.

In summary, there is a very important relationship between general vocabulary levels and competencies if one is to be successful in the process of reading. Reading ability has an important relationship to one's general level of meaning vocabulary.

PRINCIPLES FOR TEACHING VOCABULARY

If students are to build significant vocabulary skills, all instructors must incorporate and integrate various principles in carrying out the teaching program. Vocabulary skills must be developed as a result of definite, planned lessons when words are taught, explained, and reinforced, especially during the readiness stage of the content lesson. Every assignment involving either electronic or printed media creates a natural situation for vocabulary instruction.

There are at least ten important principles to remember in planning and executing lessons designed to enlarge vocabulary. These are listed and explained in the following section, and are not in any order of importance.

1. *Conduct a formal and informal assessment of all pupils' vocabulary skills to determine what kinds of teaching strategies would be most suitable for their needs.* This analysis could be undertaken through the use of formal achievement tests such as the *Iowa Tests of Basic Skills* (elementary) and the *Nelson-Denny Reading Test* (secondary). Informal devices might include cloze and maze tests (explained in an earlier chapter) as well as sentence completion tests over relevant class assignment materials. Other important instruments might include carefully constructed multiple-choice tests. The responses to these devices should provide each teacher with important data relating to each learner's present vocabulary achievement.

2. *Pre-test all students before they read a body of printed matter to gain an understanding of the specific words that must be taught and those that can be overlooked.* Every alert teacher must make a decision at the beginning of each basal reading story or content lesson regarding *which* words are absolutely vital to the subject meaning of the section. In any given class some students will know the words, some will not. Those who don't know them must be given direct lessons to aid in the meaning of the words. Those who do know them must be spared assignments that are neither relevant nor necessary for their future needs.

3. *All new and unfamiliar words should be introduced as a part of a sentence and never in isolated lists.* There are many words in the English language that must be read in a sentence in order to be pronounced and understood appropriately. Examples of these types of words are *read* and *refuse*. By using semantic clues provided by surrounding words, the task of understanding the new word is made much easier and far less complicated for the anxious learner. On the contrary, a long *list* of new words provides a rigorous challenge since there are no contextual helps available.

In every example of classroom instruction to improve vocabulary, there must be a multiplicity of methods employed. Smith, Otto, and Hansen* believe that the need is to take the time to construct lessons and motivate students to understand the concept of vocabulary development through reading, make vocabulary development part of their reading experiences, and use newly acquired words in effective reading and writing activities.

   4. *After several words have been taught, various exercises and lessons should be provided for students in order to reinforce word meanings and provide closure.* From the point of positive learning fundamentals, there is little to be gained by introducing long lists of words to readers on a daily basis and then failing to provide appropriate review and practice to reinforce the words. A few teachers engage in practices of this type by introducing "tongue twisters" and long unfamiliar words on a daily basis for the purpose of teaching "vocabulary." If there is no well-designed follow-up instruction of the words, the assignments are questionable at best. The direct attention to vocabulary should supplement vocabulary growth through reading. Thomas and Robinson** have concluded that research strongly suggests that planned instruction is superior to a casual or incidental approach.

---

*Richard J. Smith, Wayne Otto, and Lee Hansen, *The School Reading Program* (Boston: Houghton-Mifflin Company, 1978), p. 89.

**Ellen Thomas and H. Alan Robinson, *Improving Reading in Every Class* (Boston: Allyn and Baron, Inc., 1977), p. 13.

5. *Provide systematic methods for students desiring to keep a system record of the new words learned and integrated as a part of their vocabulary knowledge.* In order to develop patterns of success in corrective situations, students need to have realistic goals for learning. With respect to vocabulary enlargement, this could take the form of a vocabulary notebook in which the pupil would write down the words learned along with their appropriate definitions. If appropriate, the words could be illustrated through the use of drawings and pictures.

6. *Encourage students to participate in activities which involve wide reading from a large number of sources.* Students engaged in corrective reading programs should be given many opportunities to practice newly learned reading skills. This could be accomplished through the use of periods of uninterrupted silent reading during which each reader would have the opportunity to explore many different kinds of books and magazines that are written on various reading levels. Zintz,* for example, thinks the goal of wide reading may be accomplished by enriching the curriculum generally so that children will have much material to talk and think about. He contends that nothing can take the place of varied experience and wide reading in the building up of meanings.

7. *Teach students that single words may represent different parts of speech and have widely varying meanings depending upon their placement in the syntactical pattern of the sentence.* This goal can be accomplished through the use of crossword puzzles, multiple-choice sentences, and sentence completion exercises. Creative writing assignments entailing the use of a list of pre-taught vocabulary words may prove to be helpful. The creative use of a new illustrated, unabridged dictionary may also be appropriate for this purpose.

---

*Miles V. Zintz, *Corrective Reading*, 3rd ed. (Dubuque, Iowa: Wm. C. Brown Company, 1977), p. 419.

8. *Explain the meaning and function of Latin derivatives in order that the pupil may derive partial meaning of new words encountered in content reading.* Readers who understand that the prefix "tri" means *three* are well on their way to understanding the meaning of the word, "triglycerides." Additionally, if they understand that the term "itis" means *inflammation of,* they will know that "bronchitis" means that a person's bronchial tubes are inflammed. Thomas and Robinson* observe that nowhere do Greek and Latin word parts pay off more richly than in science. They are also valuable in mathematics and social studies.

9. *Develop the philosophy with students that because of time limitations, it is impossible to learn to recognize and derive the meanings for all unknown words.* The English language consists of literally thousands of words—many of them being unusual and a few of them of little practical use to the average reader. Students need to understand that it is possible to gather the general meaning of a sentence without knowing the exact meaning of each and every word.

10. *Give classroom lesson demonstrations involving the "hands-on" approach whereby students will come in direct contact with objects and materials representing new vocabulary words being learned.* Even though many words are easily pronounced through the use of phonic and structural analysis techniques, they do not become a part of the meaning vocabulary of an individual until they have meaning and relevance in a syntactical pattern.

Shepherd** is of the opinion that teachers should use new words repeatedly in conversation as well as in classroom

---

*Ellen Thomas and H. Alan Robinson, *Improving Reading in Every Class* (Boston: Allyn and Bacon, Inc., 1977), p. 28.
**David L. Shepherd, *Comprehensive High School Reading Methods* (Columbus: Charles E. Merrill Publishing Company, 1978), p. 47.

demonstrations. This principle is especially important when dealing with words having various shades of meaning. Additionally, this process is imperative for use with pupils learning English as a second language.

TEACHING STRATEGIES FOR CORRECTING VOCABULARY DEFICIENCIES

Two major components of vocabulary development for the disabled reader are those of diagnosis and correction. The material in this section is designed to show teachers a large number of representative activities that may be undertaken in the classroom for correcting and remediating deficiencies in vocabulary discovered as a result of applying the diagnostic procedures described in the next section of this chapter. Each of the 14 exercises in this section is designed to improve a stated significant vocabulary skill. (A valuable source book for teaching strategies dealing with vocabulary development has been published by Dale D. Johnson and P. David Pearson and is entitled *Teaching Reading Vocabulary*, Holt, Rinehart and Winston, Inc., 1978). *Reading Improvement Through Diagnosis, Remediation, and Individualized Instruction* is also useful. (See References, Note 1, p. 102.)

Exercise 1: Building Basic Vocabulary

Duplicate a selection of from 100 to 400 words (depending on the grade level of the affected students) that is at the instructional reading level of the students. The material should be of high interest to the vast majority of the pupils and contain several phrases that are at their instructional reading level. The material should be of foremost interest to a sizable group of the pupils and contain a large number of phrases that include descriptive words. After asking the students to read the material, ask each of them to complete an exercise similar to the following:

Directions:

The writer of the story you just read used many different phrases to paint a picture in the mind of you, the reader. The following expressions from "West to Kansas" add word pictures to the story and make it more interesting. Look at the list of ten expressions from the selection. On the line that follows, write another word which means the same as the underlined word. Use a dictionary if you need it.

1. Cowboys <u>cowered</u> against the wall _____
2. Jason <u>stormed</u> the assayer's office _____
3. <u>ordeal</u> dragged out for two months _____
4. <u>steep</u> prices were paid _____
5. two hundred were <u>stuffed</u> in the room _____
6. He would have his way by <u>hook or crook</u> _____
7. The rain came down in <u>buckets</u> _____
8. Many people were <u>drenched</u> _____
9. Mary <u>flew up the stairs</u> _____
10. There was a <u>maddening</u> rush of wind _____

There are numerous words in the English language that have meaning and connotations unique to a given subject area. Persons who have had very limited contact with these topics have problems on occasion understanding the meanings of these words. The pupils who have demonstrated deficiencies of this type need to participate in lessons that will help them gain necessary skill competencies. Exercise 2 is designed for the purpose of gaining experience in word meanings.

Exercise 2: Developing Word Meanings

Directions: Read the following short selection concerning cowboys of early Dodge City. Several of the words in the story are underlined. When you are through reading, write each of these underlined words on every other line on a piece of notebook paper. After each word, write what you think the word really means. Do not use the dictionary unless it is necessary.

"Cowboys of Early Dodge City"

The cowboys who lived in Dodge City in the early 1870's often wore red <u>bandannas</u> about their heads. These <u>wranglers</u> used a <u>lariat</u> to place around the necks of cattle to hold them to the ground for branding. Sometimes it was difficult to <u>lasso</u> the animals. Some calves could not find their mothers. These <u>dogies</u> were herded together and sold by <u>rustlers</u>. Nearly all cowboys wore long leather <u>chaps</u> to protect their legs from thorns and limbs.

During the spring <u>round-up</u>, the cattle were driven to market. Sometimes the animals would run in an uncontrolled manner called a <u>stampede</u>. Along the way to market the cowboys would stop their <u>chuckwagon</u> and have a meal. In many cases the cowboys had a young <u>remuda</u> boy who combed the horses to make them look clean and attractive. This was an exciting time in the history of America.

Exercise 3: Practicing New Words

In this corrective instructional game, a lingo card is constructed having the names of various words on the different squares with the word "FREE" in the middle. The words should be those recently learned in content lessons. Give a card to each pupil. Say: "I am going to read several definitions of some words. As I read a definition, place a mark on the word that represents that definition." To win the game, the student must get a whole row of words covered either horizontally, vertically, or diagonally. (A sample lingo card is shown below.)

The words used in the illustration are those normally encountered at the upper grade levels. Less difficult words should be used for pupils at lower grade levels, while multisyllabic words would be appropriate for secondary students. As a variation, deliver blank vowel lingo cards to interested students and invite them to write in words and complete lists of definitions to correlate with the words. Students could work

ILLUSTRATION

Crucial	Skill	Practical	Compose	Guide
Pride	Contain	Object	Exact	Identify
List	Provide	FREE	Factors	Capable
Special	Range	Discuss	Variety	Review
Familiar	Original	Converse	Accept	Interest

in pairs with one person acting as the player and the other as the reader of definitions. They could be rotated to various new groups to provide unlimited practice with many new words.

Exercise 4: Creating Synonyms

In this technique the teacher writes a word such as *teacher, pencil, blizzard,* and *kind* on the chalkboard or easel. Each pupil should be given a designated period of time (one or two minutes) to record as many synonyms as possible for the word. At the conclusion of the exercise, ask each pupil to read aloud the synonyms that he/she has written. The teacher should compile a composite list of synonyms offered by the total group of students. The accuracy of the words could be validated through the use of the dictionary or glossary. A variation to the activity could be undertaken by printing the names of five objects or concepts on a single line. Supply the pupils with a list of single words. Ask them to find *the* word from the list that represents the best synonym for the five words listed on a given numbered line.

Exercise 5: Building Prefixes and Suffixes

Understanding Latin prefixes and suffixes can help students enlarge total vocabularies. Many times older pupils have never learned the meaning of these affixes and are thus limited in knowing the meaning of sentences in which these words are used.

This exercise is a combination teaching-learning exercise. The first column contains the name of the prefix or suffix; the second, the meaning of the affix; and the third, a sample word. The fourth column is designed to allow readers to supply a word of their own which would be an example. Students should be allowed to use their dictionaries if desired.

PREFIXES			
Prefix	Meaning	Sample Word	Your Word
1. ex	out	excavate	
2. bi	two	bicycle	
3. sub	under	submarine	
4. dis	not	disassociate	
5. com	together	complete	
6. un	not	untie	

SUFFIXES			
Suffix	Meaning	Sample Word	Your Word
7. ful	full of	meaningful	
8. able	capable	notable	
9. less	without	worthless	
10. ist	one who	dentist	
11. itis	inflammation of	bronchitis	
12. ness	state of	preparedness	

Exercise 6: Completing Word Meanings

This exercise is a variation of the preceding activity. The student is given practice in the formation of new words which, in turn, should be of immeasurable aid to them in the building of meaning vocabulary. In this lesson the first column consists of a list of prefixes; the second column, a scrambled list of words; and the third, a space allowing the student to find a word from the scrambled list that will connect with the prefix. The following is a sample exercise. (The correct answer is listed in column 3).

Prefix	Word	Completed Word
in	seen	(inaudible)
fore	held	(foreseen)
un	spent	(unnoticed)
with	audible	(withheld)
mis	noticed	(misspent)
dis	circle	(disintegrate)
semi	curricular	(semicircle)
pre	integrate	(preclude)
extra	estimated	(extracurricular)
over	clude	(overestimated)

The students can be involved in a variation of Exercise 6. Depending on their age and maturity, they can construct exercises of their own similar to the example. An exchange of the exercises among students can take place.

Exercise 7: Extending Word Meanings

One of the goals of developmental and corrective reading is that of extending the amount of word meanings each pupil knows. The English language contains hundreds of derivations. Knowing base words and their various elements is an important step in vocabulary enlargement. This exercise consists of two columns. The first column contains a list of words with the common element, "foot,"; the second column consists of a list of scrambled meanings illustrating the definitions of the words in the first column. The student is to match the correct word with the correct meaning.

1. football	a. to put on your feet
2. footboard	b. at the base of a mountain
3. footgear	c. without a foot
4. foothill	d. the front of the stage
5. foothold	e. for use in games
6. footless	f. to hold the feet
7. footlights	g. path for people
8. footnote	h. print made by feet
9. footpath	i. a firm position
10. footprint	u. at the bottom of the page

Exercise 8: Choosing Correct Words

This exercise is a modified cloze technique and is called a "maze" procedure by some persons. The teacher should type a story or selection written at grade level difficulty. The length of the material should be from 50 to 350 words in length depending on the age and grade level of the child. Leave out every sixth word. Supply the student with a list of three possible words that may apply to a given blank. One of the words should be the word used in the original selection, another should be one that might be possible, and the third should be one that would be most inappropriate. When all students have completed the exercise, conduct an explanation of each correct answer and why the key word is the most appropriate. This corrective exercise will help the reader become more aware of contextual and general meaning clues.

Exercise 9: Building Dictionary Skills

The desk dictionary can be the source for many different types of exercises helping students to develop and correct vocabulary deficiencies. Ideally, every student in a given class should have the same, or very similar, type of dictionary for the lessons described below. Exercises such as the following might be employed:

1. Studying various multisyllabic words regarding what meaning should be attached to the various syllabic segments.

2. Interpreting the use and nature of diacritical and accent marks in helping to decide the exact meaning of words.

3. Examining the various definitions of words with the view toward selecting the one definition which applies to a word in a particular sentence.

4. Discovering how the meaning of a word changes when affixes are added to the base stem of a word.

5. Finding various synonyms and antonyms for words encountered in content reading.

Exercise 10: Understanding Word Meanings

After having studied the meaning and importance of prefixes and suffixes, the following exercise gives the student some practice in associating words with prefixes and suffixes and their proper meaning in a given sentence structure. The sample exercise might be one that would be suitable for a group of middle grade pupils.

Directions: Insert the letter of the *best* answer in the space provided.

1. *Unspent* money has _____.
   (A) been spent (B) not been spent (C) is of no value
2. A *triangle* has _____ corners.
   (A) two (B) three (C) four
3. The elections are *biennial*, therefore they are held every _____ years.
   (A) two (B) four (C) six
4. *Semiannual* programs are held _____ a year.
   (A) once (B) twice (C) four times
5. A *postscript* is written _____ of the letter.
   (A) at the beginning (B) in the middle (C) at the end

Exercise 11: Enlarging Vocabulary Skills

One of the most fascinating and interesting activities for corrective vocabulary building is the use of the crossword puzzle. Puzzles could be constructed to practice newly learned words encountered in content lesson such as science or social studies. Many of these puzzles could be constructed by the pupils themselves and exchanged with each other. The following is a sample exercise for a middle grade social studies class after the students had studied a unit on early pioneers.

	²C													
¹S	O	D	H	O	U	S	E	⁵I	N	⁶D	I	A	N	S
	³W	A	G	O	N					U				
	⁴B	L	I	Z	Z	A	R	D		S				
	O									T				
	Y													

Across: 1. Type of home built of pieces of soil.
         3. Vehicle pulled by horses.
         4. A terrible snow storm.
         5. Native Americans.
Down: 2. Person who herds cattle.
         6. A type of storm.

Exercise 12: Categorizing Common Words

This corrective vocabulary exercise gives the student review and practice in associating words in given meaning categories. The example that follows is one constructed by the author for use with upper primary and middle grade pupils. Much interesting activity can be generated by encouraging the pupils to make exercises of their own and exchanging them with fellow classmates to solve.

Directions: Below is a list of 20 words. Look at each word carefully and then write it in one of the four categories which follow:

stool	table	potatoes	plane
socks	train	car	chair
gloves	beans	bench	shoes
beets	boat	table	bus
coats	hats	beans	lettuce

Vegetables	Clothes	Transportation	Furniture

Exercise 13: Enlarging Vocabulary Through Context

One of the most important principles in teaching and learning new words is that of presenting the words in several contexts to reinforce understanding through multiple situations. In the sample exercise, the primary teacher has just completed a unit involving the neighborhood. A short review of the unit is provided. The pupils are to find the correct word from the list that should be written on the different blanks.

Directions: Read the following paragraph. Look at the list of words. Find a word from the list and write it where it belongs on the blank spaces.

We took a _____ in the neighborhood. We saw a _____ sign. We went by a _____ store. The day was _____ and windy. We walked six _____. We returned to the school building at eleven _____. The boys and girls had a _____ time.

grocery	o'clock	cold
walk	blocks	
good	stop	

Exercise 14: Building Vocabulary Through Language Experience

The use of the language-experience approach may be beneficial in building and establishing new vocabulary in a number of settings. For example, let us pretend that a brief science study has just been concluded in the area of trees. The following words and phrases have been emphasized: *evergreen, oak, bark, annual rings, maple, annual, sap*. Ask the pupils to dictate a short essay with the words included. Emphasize that they should use no more than *one* of these words in a sentence. After copying the selection on a large sheet of paper, ask selected pupils to read the story and point to the words. Students could also create stories of their own on notebook paper.

The previous 14 sample exercises represent valuable lessons for a wide range of students from the upper primary through secondary levels. Some of them will need to be adapted for use with a given group of students at a specific grade or learning level. By merely making them shorter or longer and changing the level of readability, the teacher will find that each of the suggested classroom tested exercises can be extremely useful for vocabulary enlargement.

EVALUATION OF VOCABULARY SKILL DEVELOPMENT

In order to provide a well-structured, sequential vocabulary skill program for all students, construct a carefully devised program of evaluation. There are numerous strategies for accomplishing this goal. The following informal techniques may be appropriate.

1. A list of key words is printed to the left of a page. For each key word there are four definitions. Only one definition is correct for the concerned word. The student checks the correct answer. An accuracy score of 80% should be demanded.

2. Key words and definitions are printed in two scrambled lists. The pupils match the words with the correct definitions.

In addition to the two procedures just described, there are several group commercial reading tests available for use in the evaluation of vocabulary skills. The following is a list of some of the more widely used tests.

1. *California Reading Test* (McGraw-Hill) Grades 1-14.
2. *Diagnostic Reading Tests* (Committee on Diagnostic Reading Tests) Grades K-13.
3. *Gates-MacGinitie Reading Tests* (Teachers College Press) Grades K-12.
4. *Iowa Tests of Basic Skills* (Houghton Mifflin) Grades 3-9.
5. *Metropolitan Achievement Tests:* Reading (Harcourt Brace Jovanovich) Grades 1-8.
6. *Nelson Reading Test* (Houghton Mifflin) Grades 3-9.
7. *Stanford Diagnostic Reading Test* (Harcourt Brace Jovanovich) Grades 2.5-8.5.

Information can also be obtained regarding a pupil's ability in vocabulary by carefully analyzing his/her oral and written language production. The total number of different words used in a creative essay or an extemporaneous speech is a reasonably valid index of a pupil's level of vocabulary achievement. The evaluation of the vocabulary competencies as related to any one learner is best accomplished through the use of both formal and informal test instruments on a periodic and continuous basis.

Summary

Vocabulary development is a vital ingredient in the reading program, thus, a continuing program of evaluation and ongoing instruction is both urgent and necessary. There are several types of vocabulary that are developed at various stages in the life of a given person. If these vocabularies are to be enlarged, the ten teaching principles previously described in this chapter must be observed. The 14 specific teaching strategies that have been described should be of immeasurable help in aiding children to develop and correct vocabulary skills. As noted at the end of the chapter, special attention must be given to evaluation of vocabulary.

REFERENCES

1. Cushenbery, Donald C. *Reading Improvement Through Diagnosis, Remediation, and Individualized Instruction.* West Nyack, New York: Parker Publishing Company, 1977. Ch. 2.

2. Shepherd, David L. *Comprehensive High School Reading Methods.* Columbus: Charles E. Merrill Publishing Company, 1978.

3. Smith, Richard J., Otto, Wayne, and Hansen, Lee. *The School Reading Program.* Boston: Houghton-Mifflin Company, 1978.

4. Thomas, Ellen, and Robinson, H. Alan. *Improving Reading in Every Class.* Boston: Allyn and Bacon, Inc., 1977.

5. Zintz, Miles V. *Corrective Reading* (Third Edition). Dubuque, Iowa: Wm. C. Brown Company, 1977.

4

Correcting

Word Analysis

Deficiencies of

Problem Readers

It is the feeling of many reading authorities that the process of word analysis is the center or heart of the total reading act. A reader who is successful in developing reading competencies must be able to use several different word attack techniques.

One of the principle reasons for reading deficiencies among older students is that of grave deficiencies in this important area of word analysis. There are many persons who believe that limitations in the area of phonics cripple a student's ability for later success in reading. Words must be analyzed by the reader before comprehension or reaction can take place. Word analysis is to the reading act what the human heart or circulatory system is to the human body. Before becoming concerned about comprehension and study skills, the reader must be well-trained in the area of word analysis techniques.

The material in this chapter is designed to supply important information on several topics. The first topic discussed is the place of word analysis in the total reading process. Because phonics is and has been a very controversial subject, both within and without the educational profession, the next major topic of the chapter is devoted to the importance and significance of phonics in reading and what it means to the classroom teacher at all learning levels.

Following this discussion is a list of classroom tested teaching techniques for overcoming word analysis deficiencies, especially in the areas of phonic and structural analysis.

A fourth major focus in this chapter is a description of the many classroom techniques that can be used for overcoming deficiencies in the areas of context clues and dictionary usage, especially for the middle and upper grade, and secondary school student. A summary of the material is included in the close of the chapter, along with selected references for further reading.

WORD ANALYSIS
IN THE TOTAL READING PROCESS

One of the most difficult tasks a child has to accomplish is identifying the printed symbol that stands for the spoken sound. Many children come to school at ages five and six knowing hundreds of words in their oral vocabulary; however, they are without the skills for pronouncing these words when they see them on a piece of paper. Accordingly, it is the responsibility of the teachers and the school program to provide the child with those skills that will be necessary for his/her later successes in mastering the various aspects of the reading act.

Word attack or word analysis refers to the reader's general competency in analyzing an unfamiliar word through the use of a number of strategies. The objective of learning word analysis skills is the ability to obtain meaning from the printed page. If a student is to be a proficient reader, he/she needs to gain general word attack efficiency in the important areas of phonics, structural analysis, context clues, and dictionary skills. The emphasis on each of these different skills will vary somewhat depending upon the learning level. At the primary grade level, major emphasis is given to configuration clues, picture clues, development of sight words, and basic phonics; at the upper grade and high school levels, more attention is given to context clues, structural analysis, and dictionary skills.

Obviously, an alert student does not learn all of the strategies for word analysis within the school environment.

The reader, for example, might notice words on signs that are found about the city, on the playground, or near the home. If the child has been fortunate enough to have parents or grandparents who have read to him/her, the process of word attack will be much easier for that particular reader. Words that are read and seen on the paper simultaneously provide a rich learning experience for the young child.

In attempting to determine the needs of any problem reader, one obviously must structure a meaningful program of analysis and correction for these learners. Indeed, it is vital that the structured teaching of these skills take place. If word analysis is to have its proper place in the total reading program, one must be aware of at least six important steps in accomplishing this aim.

1. *Determine which reading competencies will need to be accomplished by your students.*

As indicated in the previous chapter, the skills may be derived from a number of sources. Certainly, they should be those *you* personally feel are important to the success of reading in your particular content area. Some of these skills possibly would originate from the different areas of emphasis which are on the state-mandated competency tests. Other skill competencies might come from the school curriculum guide. Your list of required or desired competencies may be motivated by the types of employment that many of your graduates generally seek. If many of your students are directed to the professions, the ability to pronounce many difficult words in a number of different challenging materials would be very important. All of these skills that you would list for mastery learning might be stated in a behavioral sense.

2. *After having determined the list of desired word attack behaviors or skills, it is necessary to develop a strategy of assessment to determine which readers have gained these competencies and which need further help.*

The evaluation process could use a number of diagnostic instruments of both the informal and commercial type. The phonic and structural analysis tests included in the previous chapter might be a very important tool for use in this regard. Other informal techniques may consist of having the students read aloud classroom materials that are at their instructional reading levels. While the students read the material aloud, compile a miscue analysis of words that are mispronounced for any reason. After conducting the analysis of the oral reading errors, you could determine to a limited degree which students need further help in phonic and structural analysis techniques. Modified cloze techniques may be of some aid in accomplishing this goal as well.

In order to assess the strengths and limitations of each student in word attack, you should make a student profile sheet. To the left of the sheet place the names of your students; and at the top of the sheet in columns, put the names of the desired skill competencies. After having processed all of the data from the diagnostic instruments, make a checkmark in the columns for the students who need further work.

3. *An important aspect of the teacher-learning process is that of motivating the individual learner to want to improve the components of word attack.*

It is not only important to show each reader the areas of strengths and limitations, but it is also vital that the student be motivated to understand why a certain teaching program is being developed. One of the ways of doing this would be to have the affected learner listen to a tape of his/her oral reading, analyze the mistakes in the privacy of an individual conference, and demonstrate how your teaching strategies will help the student overcome these difficulties.

4. *The remediation of word attack deficiencies will come about much more quickly if the affected student can realize much success in a short period of time.*

Develop fairly short lessons of a concentrated nature

that are designed to improve one particular skill. In the case of older students, it might be an interesting lesson on the meaning of Latin prefixes and suffixes. Use a variety of teaching tools, such as the overhead projector, tape lessons, and selected workbook pages; or, if your budget permits, computer-assisted instruction for this purpose. There are a number of excellent commercial materials that are taped and are accompanied by study guides and worksheets that help the student to gain success in a brief period of time. The names of many of these materials can be found in Appendix A.

5. *After you have developed a series of lessons with a given student in a particular word attack area, it is vital that you provide meaningful practice in this skill in a natural content situation.*

It is of little use to learn new skills and then not have an opportunity to exercise them in a natural learning setting. If, for example, you have stressed the meaning and importance of Latin prefixes and suffixes, it is vital that you present a number of new words in your content lesson that have these as a part of the new words presented. From time to time, these strategies should be reviewed in a number of different situations.

6. *The word attack skills that have been taught should be evaluated on a periodic and continuous basis to determine whether or not your strategies have been helpful.*

Probably the most useful evaluation techniques would be the careful observation of oral reading or analysis of the results of a pencil and paper test. This type of test could be multiple-choice in nature. You could give, for example, three choices for how the word is broken into syllables. The student selects the choice demonstrating the correct way of dividing a particular word. In all evaluative programs, the level of the student's success or lack of success should be discussed with him/her in an individual conference. Some students with high levels of motivation may want to keep their own records and, hopefully, engage in self-diagnosis and self-analysis of their own success in accomplishing the new skills. If the classroom environment permits, it may be useful to have a small-group critique of peer performance in various situations calling for word attack proficiency.

If one is to understand the importance of word analysis in the total reading process, a number of principles of teaching these skills should be understood and inculcated in the instructional program. The principles described in this section are particularly germane to middle, upper grade, and secondary students facing competency examinations. The manner in which you approach corrective instruction in word analysis for these students is somewhat different from the general approaches you would use with younger students. If corrective instruction is approached in a rather scientific and tactful manner, students will be able to gain much proficiency in a short amount of time under your direction. The following are seven principles or guidelines you should understand and make a part of your teaching in this area for this type of student.

1. *It is important to remember that the teaching strategies for each of the older students should be on a strictly selective and individual basis.*

The more mature the student, the greater the diversity of reading abilities; thus, the instruction needed for one student certainly would not be appropriate for another. It is therefore not educationally wise to ask an entire class to complete an exercise or a lesson that may apply to only a very few students. Through the use of individual study carrels and computer-assisted instruction, this particular principle can be adhered to without much difficulty.

2. *The correction of word attack deficiencies should be thought of in the context of the total reading act.*

Phonics and structural analysis and context clues constitute only one part of reading and certainly are not the culmination of the total reading act. Therefore, word attack should take place in a meaningful context along with whatever basic comprehension skills the student may need to learn at the same time.

3. *All content teachers instructing students with word analysis deficiencies should be alert to their needs.*

The improvement of word attack skills should not occur in an isolated place under the direction of only a reading specialist. Strategies to improve word attack can be undertaken, and indeed should be stressed, by all teachers who use printed materials. There are many interesting places in social studies and science where you could demonstrate to the student how words are broken apart through structural analysis. This would be particularly true in science. If a biology teacher wanted to show the students how to pronounce "photosynthesis," this word could be taken apart and demonstrated by the teacher through the breaking down of the several syllable patterns.

4. *Students should be given training so they can use a multiple attack on unknown words.*

Proficiency in reading will come about only when students are able to use the newly learned information in their own particular reading situations in the library or at home. They should understand, for example, that they probably should use structural analysis as the first attack upon a new word and then add the phonic attack and the use of the dictionary as they become necessary. If they've had specific training in context clues, this will also be helpful in their quest to analyze the word.

5. *If the word analysis process is to have meaning for each individual student, words should be introduced within the context of a sentence or phrase.*

There is some serious question as to whether words should ever be taught in isolation. The student will need the help of surrounding words in using context clues to pronounce the word.

6. *Within the total confines of word analysis instruction as part of the reading process, the student should understand that there are no strict rules in the area of phonics and structural analysis.*

Due to the complicating factors of the structure of the English language, there are a number of so-called phonic "rules" that are taught by some teachers as if they are absolute truths. The principle of the vowel digraph where "the first vowel does the talking and the second one goes walking" is only appropriate in approximately 65-70% of those instances where there are vowel digraphs. While phonics will unlock approximately 86% of the words in the English language, there are a number of words that have high frequency in the 14% that cannot be dealt with by phonic generalizations. Therefore, the memorization of long lists of "rules" for all of the word attack behaviors would seem to have very limited, if any, use. The teacher should stress only those principles that seem to be most useful for the students.

7. *For middle, upper grade, and secondary students, the emphasis on correcting word deficiencies should probably be in the areas of structural analysis, context clues, and dictionary skills.*

Students probably have less use for phonics at these age levels. In any case, phonics instruction should be made a part of the total program for the student. If a very severe phonic deficiency is noted, all such teaching should, of course, be in an inductive manner.

Elaborate phonics programs are not appropriate for the vast majority of older readers. Assignment of extensive lessons in phonic workbooks over many hours is counterproductive to most of these students. The word attack problem of the more mature student is only a part of the general reading disability that he/she probably has.

In summary, word analysis is the heart of the total reading process and must be corrected before the student can gain success with the total reading process. There are a number of behaviors that the teacher should keep in mind when undertaking a program of word analysis correction, particularly with the older student. The central theme of these principles rests on the philosophy that the process should be a multiple approach to the skill. The older student probably has less need for phonics than the younger student; thus, unless there is a very severe deficiency, any phonics training should be only on those *generalizations* that have the most utility and are definitely needed by a given student. *Extensive* practice in phonic workbooks on the part of a *total* class cannot be justified in any well-structured corrective program.

SIGNIFICANCE OF PHONICS IN READING AND WHAT IT MEANS TO YOU

As mentioned in the previous section, phonetic analysis is an important aspect of word attack. During the first four grades of the elementary school, there is a great deal of attention given to this phase of reading instruction. The older student has been exposed to much phonic training and if he/she was a member of the low reading group in the lower grades, the learner has had a long history of exposure to different kinds of phonic lessons. The vast majority of middle, upper grade, and secondary students will probably need only a very quick review over some of the principles they may have forgotten. During the past two or three decades, there have been many kinds of phonics programs promoted in the literature. Some commercial enterprises have made it appear as if phonics is the answer to all reading problems. As indicated earlier, we should not think about phonic rules, but rather about generalizations. You would be wise to avoid using extensive phonic programs for all students in corrective reading situations. Careful analysis of the difficulties of these students would, no doubt, lead a trained reading specialist to understand that many of these students really don't need this type of instruction.

Phonics training is not an either/or situation. For the select few students who are truly deficient in this area, a series of meaningful lessons in an *inductive* manner should be presented. For students so identified, the following phonic generalizations should be taught, understood, and, eventually, used by those students who need this type of information.

1. In certain double-vowel combinations, the first vowel is usually long and the second one is silent. Examples of these would be "ay," "oa," "ai," "ee."

2. The "r" gives the preceding vowel the sound that is neither long nor short.

3. When "c" or "g" is followed by "e," "i," or "y," the sound is usually soft, such as in "city," "cycle," "gypsy," or "gist."

4. In a one syllable word, when the only vowel is at the end of the word, that letter usually stands for a long sound, such as in "he," "go," and "no."

5. A single vowel in a closed syllable usually has the short sound, such as in "met," "pet," and "cat."

6. When "c" and "h" are next to each other, they normally form only one sound. Examples of this principle are "chair" and "catch."

7. When "ght" is seen in a word, the "gh" is usually silent, such as in the words "night," and "right."

8. When two of the same consonants are side by side, only one is heard, such as in the words "miller" and "ladder."

9. When a word ends in a "vowel-consonant-e", the "e" is silent and the vowel may be long or short, such as in the words "exile," "approve," and "passage."

10. When "y" is the final letter in a word, it usually has a vowel sound, such as in the word "monkey."

The preceding list is merely a sampling of the common phonic generalizations that should be understood by all secondary students. You may wish to add others that seem applicable to your given situation.

In understanding the importance and significance of phonics to your students, be sure to keep several principles in mind. *First*, before you undertake any kind of phonics training with your students, be sure you evaluate the students' strengths and limitations in this area very carefully. There are many students who have no need for this type of training and it is a waste of time to ask them to undertake exercises that they do not need or cannot use. *Second*, phonics is only one of the fundamental word attack skills, and certainly should not be overemphasized to the exclusion of other techniques such as structural analysis, context clues, and dictionary exercises. Phonics training is most effective in the primary grades and, once a student is older, the phonic techniques have less application to his/her needs. *Third*, the value of phonic rules is highly controversial. As already pointed out in this volume, many so-called rules have limited application and should be studied and understood in that particular context. *Fourth*, precise skills training in phonic elements is not absolutely necessary for all students, since it will be necessary to teach students who have auditory handicaps to use other types of word attack techniques. Obviously, those students who have poor auditory acuity, weak auditory memory, or severe hearing problems will need types of training other than phonics. *Fifth*, there is no one particular brand of phonics that is more suitable for students than some other type. In some school systems, a particular type of phonics is being espoused as the final answer to all reading problems. *This is not so, has never been so, and will never be so.*

In summary, phonics is an important word attack skill.

For the older student, other types of word attack will probably be more important and germane. Phonics is not the absolute answer to all reading problems, and this type of training should be instituted only with those students who can demonstrate need for improving upon this type of deficiency.

CLASSROOM TESTED TEACHING TECHNIQUES FOR OVERCOMING DEFICIENCIES IN PHONIC AND STRUCTURAL ANALYSIS

In the following section, there are many interesting and worthwhile activities you can undertake with students who have severe deficiencies in either phonic or structural analysis. The exact exercises you will use with individual students depends, of course, on the students' precise needs. These are classroom tested techniques which many successful teachers have been using for some time. You will want to supplement them with some commercial materials described in the appendices section. The exercises are not presented in any particular order of importance. The items for each of the exercises have been kept rather limited in order to present as many different examples of exercises as possible. If you wish to make the exercise longer for the students whom you teach, then you will need to add similar examples.

Structural Analysis Exercises

Exercise One: Don't Let Words Trick You

Directions to the Student: There are many words in the English language often confused because of similarities in the way the words are formed. You, no doubt, know the meanings of each of the words; however, be careful when you pronounce them. Look at the syllables very carefully. Perhaps you would like to pronounce the words by using a tape recorder. Read across each row. Listen to the tape and see whether you pronounce the words correctly. Your teacher may want to listen to the tape with you to help you correct the words you may have mispronounced.

thorough	three	though	thrice
trial	trail	treed	tired
craft	crease	cease	cross
sever	seven	several	seventh
expect	suspect	except	prospect
bough	boulder	bather	bottle
easiest	earthen	easterly	earning
crank	crave	clash	crawl
lymph	luxury	lynx	lyre
mallet	malady	mallow	mammal

Each student should practice pronouncing each of the words in the ten lines until he/she is able to pronounce each word without hesitation.

Exercise Two: Can You Recognize Affixes?

Affixes are letters that are attached to the beginning or end of a word or word base to form a new word. If an affix is placed at the beginning of a root word, it is called a prefix. If an affix is placed at the end of a root word, it is called a suffix. Some of the affixes would be as follows: "ous," "er," "co," "per," "mis," "trans," "ment," "re," "ion," "de," "ful," "in," "er," and "ish."

Directions to the Student: Listed below is a column of 20 words. Using the list of affixes above, attach one of these affixes to each of the following words to form a new word. On a piece of paper of your own, write a sentence for each of your new words in which you have used the new word properly.

1. port	11. great
2. condition	12. pare
3. enlarge	13. pair
4. manage	14. match
5. proud	15. mit
6. fool	16. parch
7. plain	17. protect
8. power	18. claim
9. vent	19. lead
10. mission	20. loud

Exercise Three: Finding the Right Affix

Directions to the Student: Now that you have had practice in forming many new words by adding prefixes and suffixes, you will find ten sentences below that contain blanks. To the left of each sentence, you will see a word. Add a prefix or suffix to that word and place it in the blank in the sentence. Be sure the word you supply fits the context of the rest of the sentence.

mission	The car would not move because the _____ was broken.
managed	The store lost money because the owner _____ the account.
fool	Clowns are sometimes very _____.
pressed	He _____ a desire to go to the picnic.
danger	It is _____ to drive a car with bad tires.
condition	You can _____ a motor and make it run better.
vest	_____ in stock if you want to make a profit.
pare	_____ for the worst if you lose your job.
taken	They found the wrong person because of _____ identity.
master	He gave a _____ performance.

Exercise Four: Applying Syllabication Rules to Everyday Words

One of the problems encountered by many older students is that of applying syllabication rules to words they encounter in their everyday reading. The purpose of this classroom-tested activity is to allow the student to see the relationship between rules and everyday words they might meet.

Directions to the Student: There are a number of syllabication rules you probably already know. If you have forgotten them, let's review them again.

1. Words ending in a consonant and the letters "le" usually have a consonant begin the last syllable.
   Example: no-ble

2. A compound word is divided between the words it is composed of and between the syllables existing within these parts.
   Example: soft-ball

3. If two like consonants stand between two vowels, it is best to divide between the consonants.
   Example: nug-get

4. When two unlike consonants stand between two vowels, the word is usually divided between the consonants.
   Example: mis-take

5. When one consonant stands between two vowels, the consonant usually goes with the second vowel.
   Example: me-ter

Review these five rules very carefully and then look at the following list of words. Divide the words into syllables. If you need to look back at the five rules just stated, do so. Consult your dictionary or your teacher if you are in doubt.

1. dogcart	9. continent
2. boundary	10. pancake
3. transport	11. rider
4. canoe	12. title
5. navigate	13. perform
6. greenhouse	14. pronoun
7. lament	15. ruler
8. prospector	

Exercise Five: Practicing Your Phonetic Analysis Skills

Directions to the Student: There are many things that we know about the English language. We know that it has 26 letters in the alphabet and that they are used to spell all of the words in our language. We also know there are 43 different sounds called phonemes. They are represented by a number of different combinations of letters. If you know certain phonic generalizations, you will be able to pronounce a large number of the words in the English language. If you are an upper grade or high school student, you will remember that your elementary teacher introduced these to you. Let us now take time to review them.

1. The vowel in a syllable that ends with one or more consonants usually has a short sound. This is sometimes called a closed syllable.
   Examples: net, mat, sat, ton

2. A vowel that is the final letter is generally long. This is sometimes called an open syllable.
   Examples: be, go

3. A syllable having two vowels, one of which is the final e, generally has the long sound of the first vowel with the e being silent.
   Examples: mute, time

4. In words containing two vowels together, such as "oa," "ay," "ea," "ee," or "ai," the first one is usually long and the second one is silent. These letter combinations are called digraphs. In other words, the first letter does the talking, and the second one is silent.
   Examples: reach, train

5. Some words have a blend of two vowels that produces a glided or blended sound. These two vowels are called dipthongs.
   Examples: cow, boil

6. When c or g is followed by i, e, or y, the c or g is usually pronounced in a "soft" manner.
   Examples: city, gyp

7. When c or g is followed by a, o, or u, the c or g is usually pronounced in a hard fashion.
Examples: cow, go

8. A vowel in an unaccented syllable will have what we call the schwa sound. This sound is not distinct and is different from most other sounds. In the dictionary, the schwa sound is designated by the inverted e.
Examples: circus, about

Now that we have reviewed the phonic principles, let us see if we can apply them to certain common words. You will find five words listed after each number below. In the blank following the last word, put the number of the principle above that illustrates the sound of the words listed.

1. straight, stay, tree, throat, ray _____
2. boycott, mouth, flower, broil, trout _____
3. dresser, endeavor, gardener, graven, maritime _____
4. mode, cube, precede, live, tripe _____
5. gyrate, gypsy, century, cent, cyst _____
6. cough, calculate, got, gave, gourd _____
7. bud, ash, mat, pat, mit _____
8. to, me, go, villi, zero _____

Exercise Six: What Do You Remember About Phonics and Structural Analysis?

Directions to the Student: We have been studying various aspects of phonics and structural analysis. This exercise will help you decide whether or not you understand all the principles you should remember about these two important word attack tools. Below are two lists. The first list, numbered 1-10, contains items that we have studied. The second list, lettered a-l, contains words that represent these aspects. Use this matching exercise to see if you have mastered these skills. The list of words contains two more words than there are items in the first column, so be very careful when you make your choices.

A WORD THAT CONTAINS:

____	1. a prefix, root word, and suffix	a.	meat
____	2. a dipthong	b.	about
____	3. a digraph	c.	certain
____	4. an open syllable	d.	matador
____	5. a schwa sound	e.	Mississippi
____	6. a soft "c" sound	f.	predict
____	7. a hard "g" sound	g.	unfaithful
____	8. three syllables	h.	met
____	9. a prefix meaning "before"	i.	cultivate
____	10. a closed syllable	j.	bout
		k.	gravel
		l.	me

IMPROVING READING COMPETENCIES
IN DICTIONARY SKILLS AND CONTEXT CLUES

Despite the fact that the dictionary has been a source book for use in schools many years, far too many students have not learned how to use this important source in a correct manner. Even though dictionary skills are normally taught at the elementary levels; middle and upper grade students as well as high school students need further refinement in this important area. Typically, these students need further practice in such aspects as alphabetical sequence, phonetic spellings (such as the use of diacritical marks), and finding the correct definition for a given word. Any student not functioning in these areas needs further practice.

Context clues constitute one of the most important techniques for use by high school students in analyzing a word. Understanding the relationship among known and unknown words is an important attitude and/or skill to be developed. The exercises in the latter part of this section are classroom tested and are designed to help those students who need further aid in refinement of this skill.

Exercise One: Alphabetizing

Directions to the Student: Number each column of words in the order in which you would find the words in the dictionary.

___ eventful	___ percolate	___ nebula	___ snipe
___ eucalyptus	___ mental	___ notation	___ mirage
___ endeavor	___ heritage	___ nook	___ ovation
___ evict	___ reckon	___ nature	___ scarf
___ exalt	___ sculptor	___ nurse	___ physical
___ encore	___ jeep	___ nutrient	___ lack
___ endue	___ gout	___ nail	___ neck
___ excite	___ outpour	___ nomad	___ lacking
___ emit	___ scrawl	___ okra	___ overbear
___ extricate	___ battery	___ official	___ flute

Exercise Two: Can You Use Guide Words?

Directions to the Student: At the top of each dictionary page you will find two guide words. These guide words are the first and last words on that page. If you use guide words correctly, they will help you to discover if the word you are looking for is on that particular page. Therefore, you must make a decision as to whether the word that you have in mind is located alphabetically between the first and the second guide word. Below you will find two columns. Column one contains a list of guide words. In column two, you will find four words. Draw a line under the *one* word that can be found on the page where the guide words occur.

Column One	Column Two
1. foam - follow	flume, fatigue, folio, flux
2. greet - grind	grin, graze, ginger, glacier
3. importer - imprint	imprudent, impostor, infant, imply
4. limbo - linear	limp, lisp, lien, licorice
5. molasses - monastic	mongrel, monk, monarch, moist
6. flimsy - Florence	floor, flounce, firefly, flaccid
7. gamekeeper - garnet	gambler, garrison, gargle, gazelle
8. haw -headfirst	heart, harmful, haven, header
9. northerner - note	not, northern, norm, north
10. pinion - piston	pitcher, pit, pinhole, pinto

Exercise Three: Practice Sounds of Word Parts

Directions to the Student: As you look at words and their definitions in the dictionary, you will find a number of pieces of information given. For example, you will find how the word is to be accented. You will also discover information as to how the word is to be divided into the various syllables; what the vowel sound of each accented syllable is; and any information relating to the schwa sound of the syllables.

Below is a list of twenty words. Write these words on a piece of paper and complete the following information about each word.

 a. Mark the primary and secondary accents.

 b. Indicate the vowel sounds of each of the accented syllables.

 c. Divide the word into syllables.

 d. Indicate the schwa sound if it is present in the word.

 e. Indicate the part or parts of speech the word represents.

1. carpenter	11. mathematics
2. Christianity	12. moratorium
3. conservative	13. oracle
4. desirability	14. pituitary
5. domesticate	15. pretentious
6. ganglion	16. pyorrhea
7. hieroglyphic	17. recurrence
8. inclination	18. reassurance
9. innumerable	19. ruminate
10. lamentable	20. spaghetti

You may wish to exchange your paper with one of your classmates for scoring or, if directed, give your lesson to your teacher for scoring.

Exercise Four: Finding the Right Word in Context

Directions to the Student: Many words in the English language look alike. A change in a single letter can change the whole meaning of a word. You need to look very carefully to see if the word fits in the context of a particular sentence.

Below are ten sentences. Locate the misused word. On the first blank following the sentence, write the misused word. On the second line, write the word you think belongs in the sentence.

---

1. Marie sank a song at the beginning of the program.

   _____   _____

2. All of the soft drinks had been put in battles.

   _____   _____

3. Mr. and Mrs. Jones placed a "For Scale" sign in their front yard.

   _____   _____

4. Mother baked a cheery pie for the picnic supper.

   _____   _____

5. The lovely sweater John bought for the dance had begun to shriek.

   _____   _____

6. We bought five quarts of milk at the Adams Country Diary.

   _____   _____

7. The entire family spent two days at the State Fare.

   _____   _____

8. We read our male when we got it from the post office.

   _____   _____

9. The heathen tribes worshiped an ideal during each noon meal.

   _____   _____

10. We all wore mashes in the three act play.

   _____   _____

Exercise Five: Can You Find The Right Word?

Directions to the Student: One of the ways your teacher has of finding out how well you know proper words in context is to use a cloze test. This involves taking a series of sentences and leaving out every fifth word. If you can discover the correct word to go in each of the blanks, you may have good knowledge of context clues. Below is a story about the Pacific Ocean. Every fifth word is left out. There are 20 blank spaces.

Below the story, you will find numbers 1-20. After each number there are three words. *One* of the words is the *correct* word to go in the blank. The other two are not useful for that particular blank. Write down the *correct* word for each of the blanks.

The Pacific Ocean covers _____ (1) one-third of the _____ (2) surface and at one _____ (3) is over 36,000 feet _____ (4). The Pacific contains a _____ (5) of inlet seas such _____ (6) the Sea of Japan _____ (7) the Coral Sea. The _____ (8) part of the ocean _____ (9) off the coast of _____ (10). There are numerous kinds _____ (11) currents in the ocean. _____ (12) are warm and some _____ (13) cold. The winds that _____ (14) over the ocean vary _____ (15) intensity from tradewinds _____ (16) typhoons. The Pacific Ocean _____ (17) a huge body of _____ (18) covering over 60 million _____ (19) miles. It is nearly _____ (20) the size of any other ocean on the surface of the world.

1.	contains	approximately	somewhat
2.	state's	water	world's
3.	point	island	deep
4.	out	deep	across
5.	yard	number	mile
6.	as	and	rivers
7.	across	and	to
8.	deepest	best	narrowest
9.	and	the	is
10.	Egypt	Asia	Iowa
11.	of	and	an
12.	one	none	some
13.	is	might	are
14.	freeze	blow	train
15.	in	and	of
16.	an	to	Asia
17.	moves	is	lifts
18.	rocks	air	water
19.	and	square	many
20.	almost	twice	one
			thousand

Exercise Six: More Practice with a Cloze Story

Directions to Student: Below is another selection using the cloze procedure described in the preceding activity. Every fifth word has been left out of the selection. All of the words have been placed in a scrambled list at the end of the selection. Some of the words occur more than once. Find the right word from the list and write it in the blank where it belongs.

The river city of ____ (1), Nebraska was founded in ____ (2), just before the Civil ____ (3). The next year, 1855, ____ (4) was designated the capitol ____ (5) the Nebraska territory; however, ____ (6) in 1867, the capitol ____ (7) moved to Lincoln where ____ (8) is now located.

From ____ (9) to the present, Omaha ____ (10) grown steadily in population ____ (11) the latest census indicates ____ (12) the city and surrounding ____ (13) may contain 500,000 people. ____ (14) the late 1800's, Omaha ____ (15) a leading city on ____ (16) Union Pacific. Today it ____ (17) the headquarters for the ____ (18) Pacific Railroad Company. Early ____ (19) this century, Father Flanagan's ____ (20) Boystown was established just west of Omaha.

in	is	area	in	of
Union	the	that	became	1854
has	War	and	Omaha	it
was	1854	later	it	famous

The numerous classroom tested activities included in the preceding section should be of much help to your students as they prepare for the important area of word attack on local and state-mandated competency tests. As previously indicated, you may wish to make the exercises longer, shorter, easier, or more difficult, depending on the level of students with whom you are working. The exercises formulated in this chapter have been used by literally dozens of successful teachers. Give them a try today and discover the positive results in the reading skill growth of your students.

Summary

Word attack is the heart of the reading act. Students who expect to have success in reading must develop a high level of competency with regard to all facets of this important skill segment. There are numerous principles you should keep in mind as you help students in the correction of word analysis difficulties. Word analysis is only one part of the total reading process and should always be thought of in that particular way.

The subject of phonics has been a controversial issue for decades. The use of phonetic analysis tools can help the reader analyze approximately 86% of the words in the English language. Therefore, a reader who does not have phonics skills will be severely handicapped. The classroom tested activities included in this chapter relating to phonic analysis, structural analysis, dictionary usage, and context clues, should provide much practical help to all teachers who need ready and meaningful practice for those students deficient in these areas.

REFERENCES

1. Bond, Guy L., Tinker, Miles A., and Wasson, Barbara B. *Reading Difficulties: Their Diagnosis and Correction.* Englewood Cliffs, N. J.: Prentice-Hall, Inc., 1979. Ch. 9-10.
2. Burns, Paul C. and Roe, Betty D. *Teaching Reading in Today's Elementary Schools.* Chicago: Rand McNally College Publishing Company, 1980. Ch. 3.
3. Cheek, Martha Collins and Cheek, Earl H., Jr. *Diagnostic-Prescriptive Reading Instruction.* Dubuque, Iowa: Wm. C. Brown Company, 1980. Ch. 10.
4. Hill, Walter R. *Secondary School Reading: Process, Program, Procedure.* Boston: Allyn and Bacon, Inc., 1979. Ch. 10.
5. Thomas, Ellen Lamar and Robinson, H. Alan. *Improving Reading in Every Class.* Boston: Allyn and Bacon, Inc., 1977. Ch. 2.

5

Building Reading

Comprehension

and Study Skills

Probably the most important aspect of the reading act is comprehension. While the heart of the reading act is word analysis or word recognition, the purpose of the process is to understand and comprehend those words that have been analyzed. Many persons believe that if children can use phonics appropriately and know all the rules of phonics and structural analysis, they can perform at a very high level of reading proficiency. Unfortunately, in every school there are a few students who are excellent word callers but are unable to tell the teacher what they have read.

Comprehension is an extremely complex process and involves a number of subskills. There are at least twelve of these subskills that may be grouped into four different levels. Students need to be given very precise lessons in the building of these various comprehension skill strengths.

The purpose of this chapter is to provide specific information and meaningful discussion relating to six important aspects of the total process of developing comprehension and study skills. These topics are: the meaning of comprehension; factors involved in comprehension abilities; the four levels of comprehension; principles and procedures for measuring comprehension and study skills; fifteen effective methods for building comprehension skills; and procedures for developing study skills. The diagnostic and corrective teaching exercises described in this chapter have been thoroughly classroom

tested by dozens of highly successful teachers at all grade
levels. If you have problem readers in your classroom needing
specific help in comprehension, the information in this chapter
is especially designed for your use.

WHAT READING COMPREHENSION MEANS

Reading is one of the most demanding tasks a child is
asked to perform. While a young child comes to school at the
kindergarten or first grade level speaking hundreds of words,
the most immediate challenge for the learner is finding the
printed word that stands for the spoken sound. The innovative teacher uses the various word analysis techniques to help
accomplish this goal. These techniques include such aspects as
phonics, structural analysis, context clues, sight word vocabulary, and the use of the dictionary. After all of these skills
have been developed, the reading act is still incomplete. The
reader must not only pronounce the word silently or orally,
but also must convey the meaning of the word. Comprehension of the information is evaluated by most teachers by asking oral or written questions. Many students have difficulty
with comprehension because of any one or more of the different factors that are discussed in the next section.

There are numerous skills that should be mastered in the
area of comprehension. If you are to develop a meaningful
instructional program in comprehension for your students, a
number of basic principles must be remembered.

1. *A comprehension skill program must be very care-*
   fully planned and constructed, and in sequential or-
   der.

There are at least four major levels of comprehension
skills, thus each teacher must determine well in advance of
each school year which subskills under each level would be
appropriate for the students. For example, at the primary
grade level, the major emphasis would be on reading to understand details and to get main ideas, and on using the context clues. At the upper grade and high school levels, more

attention will be given to the critical and creative levels of comprehension involving critical reading and identifying propaganda techniques.

Young children should develop skills early in the reading program with respect to understanding the meanings of single words, phrases, sentences, and short paragraphs. By the time children reach the middle and upper grade levels, they should be able to understand the meanings of several pages or a unit. Senior high students should be able to read a complete chapter and understand the main principles involved. College and university level students should be able to read complete books or parts of books, make comparisons, and show proficiency at higher levels of comprehension skill development.

Many comprehension skills are common to several learning levels. Students in all grades have need for reinforcement and correction exercises dealing with such subskills as main ideas, predicting outcomes, and following the author's intent. An ongoing program must be maintained as well for the continued development of literal skills, such as following directions. Many older students and adults find the task of following directions a very difficult challenge. They have problems with reading and following recipes; understanding the material relating to details of traffic regulations (as they study for driver's license examinations); or assembling a gift, such as a bicycle or a bookshelf, for a friend.

In order to carry on this type of sequential program of comprehension development, one needs to diagnose each student's abilities in the various comprehension skill areas. An item analysis of these various skills should be made for each learner and a program of prescriptions and lessons should be undertaken to help the student improve in the areas of limitation. Practical suggestions relating to both diagnostic and corrective teaching strategies are included in later material in this chapter.

2. *The total area of comprehension skill development must be thought of in global terms instead of a single*

skill component such as reading and remembering details.

The total act of comprehension consists of at least nine different aspects. These include looking for and remembering specific facts; locating main ideas; understanding a sentence and paragraph; sequencing, using the context as a key to comprehension; drawing conclusions; recognizing emotional reaction; inferring traits of the various characters; and understanding the intent of the author. In addition to these, one might well add such aspects as reading maps, graphs, and charts; reading to summarize and organize; understanding the sequence of events; and reading to predict outcomes. Each of these various areas also has a number of different skill competencies which are unique to it.

As one can see, the ability to comprehend information involves a number of processes and skills. Effective teachers who understand the process prepare lessons and exercises that will evaluate each student's ability to function in these skills at appropriate learning levels. Reading and remembering minute details to be "parroted" on a test is obviously only one very small part of the total comprehension process.

3. *Materials used for the building of comprehension skills should be at the instructional reading level of the learner and represent a wide variety of stories and other types of information.*

Printed materials used for comprehension skill development should be at the instructional reading level of the learner using the instructional aid. At this level the student is able to pronounce at least 95% of the words when reading aloud, and has overall comprehension of at least 75% of the material when reading silently. For older students, this means that teachers would need to have a wide variety of materials available to meet the needs of those at varying reading levels. In a typical classroom, one can take ⅔ of the mean chronological age of the learners present and gain some idea of the range of reading levels. In a high school sophomore class where the mean chronological age may be fifteen, one might find as many as ten different reading levels present. If indeed this is the case, teachers of heterogeneous groups at this chronological age level would need to have reading materials in a wide variety of categories and at many different reading levels if students are to read and, indeed, comprehend the material appropriately. Students greatly deficient in reading may well need a number of high interest-low vocabulary books. Several publishers, including Follett Publishing Company and Globe Publishing Company, print books that have interest levels for the older student but with readability at about the 5th and 6th grade levels. These books would be especially helpful for high school students who are deficient readers. There are many suggestions by the authors of these and related materials for helping pupils with comprehension difficulties.

4. *If the total comprehension process is to be meaningful for the student, the teaching-learning program for each learner must include a constant program of review and reinforcement.*

There is no place in the reading curriculum where one can stop teaching a skill simply because it is thought that the student has mastered this particular aspect of comprehension. Reading for details and main ideas is not to be taught and learned only at the primary grade levels. These skills need to be reinforced and strengthened at all learning levels, including college. Many adults are unable to follow directions appropriately, remember details, or discern a main idea. The innovative, effective teacher will make an analysis of each student's comprehension abilities, take the learner where he/she is with respect to the skills, and conduct a meaningful ongoing program of diagnosis and correction.

5. *The process of comprehension should be undertaken in a number of settings, including silent and oral reading.*

While the major emphasis of this chapter is on the diag-

nostic and corrective techniques for helping a student build
and/or correct reading skills, one must not forget that listening comprehension is also very important. Many older students and adults learn a very high percentage of their facts
and general knowledge by listening to television, teacher lec-
tures, and recordings or other media items. Therefore, comprehension takes place in a number of settings. Some students are effective in comprehension in both silent and oral
reading situations, while others are not. There are a number
of significant factors related to effective comprehension.
These aspects are discussed in the next section.

FACTORS INVOLVED
IN COMPREHENSION ABILITIES

Since I conduct many reading workshops for teachers
across the country each year, I very frequently ask participants to list those topics on which they would like specific
information. At the top of most lists I find, "How can I help
my students remember what they read?" Teachers lament
that many of their students in the upper grades and high
school cannot remember simple details for a test. They fear
for their futures as they prepare for local and state mandated
competency tests. Several years ago I conducted a survey of
the most significant reading problems of university freshmen.
The overwhelming response was "I cannot remember what I
have read." Many of these students appear to have average to
above-average levels of intelligence. Most of them come from
socioeconomic backgrounds normally thought to be very appropriate and advantageous. Many of them appear very eager
to learn. Some of them have felt so concerned about reading
problems that they've enrolled in commercial speed-reading
courses hoping this activity would help them with comprehension.

For one or many reasons, these students have not con-
quered the formidable task of developing a suitable level of
comprehension. Therefore, interested teachers should understand the factors that relate to comprehension and make both

formal and informal assessments as to how these factors relate to any one given student's comprehension strengths or difficulties.

A substantial amount of evidence indicates that there is no one factor that causes disability in reading. This is especially true about comprehension deficiencies. A given student's difficulties in the comprehension of material may be the result of any one or all of the factors described in this section.

1. Background

One of the chief difficulties for many students in determining the meaning of a word is lack of background. Some students have much proficiency in analyzing words through the use of phonics, but they have no way of determining what the word means after they have pronounced it. They have not had prior experience with a word and have no way of knowing what the word might mean. Perhaps they've had limited experience, lacking field trips or a rich socioeconomic environment that might have allowed them to come in contact with many words and concepts. If they have not read widely, it is possible that they have never encountered a given word before.

There are several ways of determining the impact of a lack of experience on a given student's reading difficulties. One may wish to use the cloze test to determine whether or not a student can understand a given word. The test results from various reading achievement measures may give a cue as to whether or not a given learner has a background for understanding a word. A careful analysis of a student's writing projects may lend some information relevant to his/her background of understanding. The careful analysis of a given student's oral language during day-to-day conversations will also lend some information relative to this factor.

Students deficient in experience will need some intensive lessons in the general areas of vocabulary and readiness for the reading act. The use of print and non-print aids may be quite helpful. Stimulating bulletin boards calling attention to

new words may be an innovative way of building meaning for
words. Other techniques might include the use of filmstrips,
films, and resource speakers. Field trips to museums, zoos,
and factories may also be helpful in building a background for
words and concepts.

2. Physical Factors

There may be a positive relationship between physical
factors and comprehension abilities in many circumstances.
Students who have great difficulties in the areas of comprehension should certainly receive a very thorough physical examination to determine if any problems such as inadequate
eyesight, defective hearing, or glandular disturbances may
exist. There are more students in this country who are un-
dernourished than was once thought. Certainly a student who
is hungry or cold will not be in a suitable mood to understand
the material in a third-hour history class. Due to the fact that
illegal drug use and, especially, marijuana usage has doubled
in recent years, the effect of drugs on the physical nature of
older students may be a significant factor in comprehension.
To remember what is read is a complex task and demands
that all facets of a physical being be at satisfactory levels. All
students who have any type of physical problem should be
referred to school or community health agencies for help with
the problem. For those students whose families have financial
problems, various civic groups such as the Kiwanis and Ro-
tary Clubs regularly supply funds for hearing aids, eye
glasses, milk, and hot lunches. The Shriners organization
sponsors hospitals for crippled children. Those who are unable to pay may go to these hospitals without charge. In
summary, a student's physical problems must be remedied
before serious attention can be given to correcting comprehension deficiencies.

3. Emotional Factors

Of all of the factors related to effective comprehension,
the emotional status of a student may be one of the most

important. At the present time, pressure on young children and older students appears to be at an all-time high. Traumatic events, such as the separation of the various family members, divorce, terminal illness, unemployment, and general political unrest may be very disturbing to many students. Even though a given learner may have an adequate level of intelligence and be physically healthy, he/she will not be able to remember main ideas and details in the second hour biology class if he/she has observed a serious quarrel between mother and father before breakfast on a particular day. A child who is not wanted by the family has little motivation to comprehend any type of reading material. Child abuse appears to be at an epidemic level in this country. Some authorities state that a child dies every four hours in the United States as a result of reported child abuse. It is unknown how many thousands of cases occur and are *not* reported to the authorities. All of these conditions can have a very serious impact on a student's ability to comprehend material.

If you are to help a student who has severe comprehension difficulties, it will be necessary to make a study relating to any emotional problems that the learner might have. In order to gather this type of information, it may be necessary to enlist the aid of school counselors, psychologists, and psychiatrists from public and private agencies. While it is assumed that you may not have direct impact on resolving the emotional problems of a student; you, nevertheless, need to be aware of these factors in order to understand exactly what kinds of comprehension exercises and techniques are needed.

4. General Level of Intelligence

There tends to be a positive relationship between overall achievement in comprehension and general level of intelligence, especially in adolescents. Some of the same qualities that are demanded on achievement tests are also required on comprehension exercises. These would involve such aspects as generalizing, comparing, contrasting, and evaluating. Some individual intelligence tests contain subsections that

deal with reasoning power and are verbally loaded. Students
who lack a general background of understanding for words
and have many problems in the area of comprehension are
unable to function well on these tests.

In undertaking an analysis of the comprehension abilities
of students, it would be well to get a general impression as to
the overall level of general mental ability the learner possesses. While intelligence tests have many limitations, they give
a general score with regard to the possible abilities of students in performing mental tasks. The best types of intelligence tests for use with students having comprehension problems are those that have a performance section, such as the
Wechsler Intelligence Scale for Children. One should avoid
the use of scores from group intelligence tests since these
data appear to be more of a reflection of a given student's
reading ability than his/her own general level of intelligence.

5. Word Analysis Skills

Obviously, a student must be in a position to analyze a
word through phonics, structural analysis, context clues, and
the use of the dictionary before attempting to determine the
meaning of the given word. Therefore, students who have a
great deal of difficulty pronouncing very simple words will
also have trouble in such literal comprehension tasks as reading to remember details or deriving a main idea. Thus, in
establishing the priority of correcting reading skills for a very
deficient reader, one should probably concentrate on trying to
correct severe word analysis deficiencies before undertaking
a long series of lessons to improve comprehension.

There are several excellent commercial tests available
for measuring word attack skills such as the *McCullough
Word Analysis Test*, the *Doren Diagnostic Test*, the *Diagnostic Reading Scales*, and the *Gates-McKillop Reading Diagnostic Test*. Having a given student read aloud while making a
very careful recording of the oral mistakes may be quite useful as well. For an exact evaluation of oral miscues, you may

wish to avail yourself of Dr. Kenneth Goodman's* *Miscue Analysis Techniques.*

6. Lack of Purpose for Reading

Some reading authorities feel that lack of purpose for reading may well be one of the most significant factors related to ineffective comprehension. Imagine the trauma of readers who are told that they will be given a final test over the entire textbook, three other related textbooks, and anything that the teacher has said during the entire school year. This type of comprehension test could be horrifying if given to students with comprehension problems. Students who lack a purpose for reading will probably comprehend very little of the material, even though they may have high levels of intelligence and be gifted readers otherwise.

It behooves every teacher who uses printed materials to always give students a purpose for reading before any kind of assignment is given. The questions or purposes assigned a student may come from three different sources: the teacher, the author of the printed material, or indeed, the students themselves. It is hoped that purposes and questions will present a number of different types of comprehension questions from each of the four levels: literal, interpretative, critical, and creative.

In summary, there are several factors related to ability to comprehend. Each student who has a serious deficiency in comprehension should be assessed to see which of these aspects are related to his/her problems. Some of the factors, such as experience, word analysis skills, and purpose for reading can be aided by the thoughtful teacher.

THE FOUR LEVELS OF COMPREHENSION

Though most reading specialists concede that comprehension is a complex concept and involves many skills, there

---

*Kenneth S. Goodman, "A Linguistic Study of Cues and Miscues in Reading," *Elementary English*, 42 (October, 1965) pp. 639-643.

is some agreement that there are at least four general levels
of comprehension. These levels are literal, interpretative,
critical and creative. Proficiency in all four of the levels is
urgent and necessary for any accomplished reader. No one of
the levels is more important than any other and each should
be given equal attention by innovative and effective teachers.
Generally speaking, more emphasis is given in the primary
and middle grades to literal and interpretative levels of comprehension, whereas more attention is typically given to critical and creative reading at the upper grade and secondary
levels. Older students who have deficiencies in literal and
interpretative comprehension will obviously need additional
corrective lessons in those areas as well. The purpose of this
section is to describe briefly these four levels and what they
mean to a general program of comprehension skill development.

1. Literal Comprehension

The lowest level of comprehension is usually called literal
comprehension and involves what readers do when they respond to material with a large number of details or facts. The
most basic level of literal comprehension is called reproduction. In these situations, the reader merely names or lists
details which have been read a very short time before. In
other words, the reader reproduces what the author says and
does without any interpretation or evaluation of the material.
If the reader desires to paraphrase the words of the author,
this might be called the translation level.

In an American history class, the following questions
would be representative of questions at the literal level of
comprehension.

1. Who was the Secretary of State for President William
   McKinley?
2. When was Oklahoma admitted as a state?
3. Who were the candidates for President in the election
   of 1932?

4. How many different presidents have served the United States since 1940?

5. What is the name of the present Secretary of Defense?

Unfortunately, literal questions involving reproduction and translation receive a disproportionate amount of attention from many teachers and textbooks. Even at the college level, many instructors are guilty of asking long lists of test questions that involve merely the meaningless reproduction of insignificant details from the textbook. While remembering details and directions is certainly important to many subject areas, the entire concept of comprehension involves much more than this particular ability. Students in such areas as social studies, literature, and science must be encouraged and helped to read efficiently at the interpretative, critical, and creative levels as well. This particular goal would be especially urgent for average and above-average readers; however, even those students who are reluctant readers should be encouraged to participate in the higher levels of comprehension.

2. Interpretative Level of Comprehension

The interpretative level of comprehension is also sometimes known as inferential comprehension. Involved in interpretative comprehension would be inference subskills such as interpreting what is read, drawing conclusions, summarizing, reading between the lines, sensing the author's mood and purpose, predicting outcomes, and analyzing the overall intent of the writer. At the interpretative level, readers merely interpret what they think the writer is trying to say without making a value judgment about whether the material may be factual or opinionated.

In the American history class cited previously, the teacher may ask the following questions that would be representative of the interpretative level of comprehension.

1. According to the author of the text, what was one of

the major reasons for American involvement in the War of 1812?

2. What were three major reasons for the people wanting to go west in covered wagons during the 1870's?

3. Were there other reasons for the War Between the States besides the issue of slavery?

4. Why do you suppose so many soldiers deserted the Confederate and Union armies in the War Between the States?

5. Why do you think car manufacturers want a limit on foreign imports?

The kinds of questions just cited call for some serious thinking on the part of the learner beyond the literal level of comprehension. This is a very important skill because many of the school, out-of-school, and job related tasks of the student call for reading between the lines. Sometime, sooner or later, the learner will have to decide what the author is really trying to say. In other words, the student should be able to write down what the "moral of the story" might be.

There are many opportunities in all content areas to ask interpretative level questions. One should require written and oral answers to interpretative questions that might be given in class and for out-of-class reading assignments. While the more able students probably will have very little difficulty with this type of question, the less able learners should also be expected to deal with this kind of task within the bounds of their abilities.

3. Critical Reading

There are many students who appear to function very well at the literal and interpretative levels of comprehension but fail to function at a satisfactory level in critical reading skills. Critical reading skills involve such things as identifying propaganda techniques and determining if a statement is a fact or an opinion. In other words, the reader has read the material and is making a determination as to whether or not the printed matter is relevant, factual, and germane based on his/her background. The reader makes a value judgment about the worth of the material in a given situation.

The following are examples of questions at the critical reading level.

1. On page 49, the author of our text says that Wisconsin has the best climate of any state in America. From what you know about the climate in the various states of our country, are you prone to believe that the statement is a fact or an opinion?

2. According to a survey by a leading athletic shoe manufacturer, three out of four teenagers buy and wear Best Wear shoes. Based on this information, do you think you should buy a pair of Best Wear shoes?

3 From what you have heard, do you think it was wise for the United States to attempt to rescue the hostages in Iran?

4. Why do you think Congress passed a law stating that a President could not serve for more than two terms?

5. Senator Knowitall said yesterday that the leading cause of the high crime rate in this country is unemployment. From what you have heard or read, do you think that this statement is a fact or an opinion?

You must understand that students will not read at the critical level unless they are required to do so. Students in a democratic society such as the United States should be able to think and read critically and make value judgments of their own. If they are unable to do this, they obviously will be persuaded to buy products and ideas which are not desired or needed. Persons who use "high pressure" techniques to sell products and ideas will find these individuals gullible and easily swayed to their product or viewpoint. If this situation is to be altered, you and all other teachers must insist that readers deal with critical reading comprehension questions. Obviously, students will not analyze propaganda techniques for "bandwagon effect" or the "plain folks device" if they are not required to do so. If the only purpose of the teacher is for a literal reproduction of facts for a test, that will be the only level on which students will operate. Effective reading instruction dictates that all teachers ask questions of students involving all four levels of comprehension.

4. Creative Reading

The highest level of reading involves creative reading skills. At the creative level, the reader has read the information from a printed source, has been able to reproduce the details, made some conclusions relative to the main idea, and has been able to differentiate bewteen fact and opinion. Now the most important question becomes, "What does this information say to me? How will I change my life or my thinking about something as a result of having read this information?"

Effective advertisers hope that all persons who read their advertising copy will read at the creative reading level. It does little good for people to read and understand a piece of advertising and then not make a decision to buy the product which has been described. The only profitable and useful aspect of advertising for the business is when customers pass through the door and buy *their* products.

The following questions may well represent the creative comprehension level.

1. If you had been Mayor Smith, would you have run for a second term?

2. If you were the librarian of this school, would you have an amnesty day when persons could bring back overdue books without paying fines? Why or why not?

3. Some government officials feel there should be no import quotas and that foreign manufacturers should be able to send as many cars as they want to America for sale at lower prices than American-made cars. As a result, many American car factories had to close and people have been put out of work. Do you think that

this situation is fair to the American worker? Why or why not?

4. In the play we have just read, Annabelle said that she didn't think she had to support her family. Do you think she had a reason to make this statement?

5. Most farmers produce more grain and other products than they can use themselves. Do you think the State and Federal governments are responsible for assuring that the farmers make a profit on their products?

The assigning of creative level questions to students calls for much innovation on the part of the teacher. Typically, these kinds of questions are not given on tests because they have much less objectivity than a factual type question and therefore are much more difficult to grade and evaluate. It behooves every teacher, however, to give students the chance to relate and to state their feelings with regard to the types of materials that they read. As students leave our secondary schools, they certainly will need to possess creative reading skills in order to make responsible decisions for themselves. Without this ability, they will make many wrong decisions in such important areas as buying products, selecting a marriage partner, or joining a church or political party.

You must remember that a significant part of mandated competency tests will involve questions related to comprehension. Typically, these tests involve short selections with various types of questions that follow. Many of these are at the literal level; however, some are at the interpretative and creative reading levels as well. In order to help ensure that your students pass these examinations, it is imperative that you give them practice and help in dealing with questions at the four levels just discussed.

PRINCIPLES AND PROCEDURES
FOR MEASURING COMPREHENSION AND STUDY SKILLS

If one is to construct an effective program of comprehension skill development, it is necessary to evaluate each student's abilities with respect to the skills involved at the four levels of comprehension. There are numerous ways of accomplishing this type of diagnostic program. Listed below are several different alternatives for assessing comprehension and study skills development. You, no doubt, will want to use a combination of these practices and procedures rather than employing any one of them on an exclusive or sole basis.

1. *There are a number of standardized achievement tests that measure comprehension abilities.*

Some of these include the *Gates-MacGinitie Reading Tests* which extend from elementary through the high school level. The *Iowa Test of Basic Skills* is an excellent test for evaluating comprehension. The publishers of the *Iowa Test* will also supply an item analysis with respect to the various comprehension skills if this is desired by a particular school system. The *Nelson-Denny Reading Test*, which is useful at the high school and college levels also, evaluates various comprehension skill strands. There are also comprehension sections on various individual diagnostic reading tests, such as the *Durrell Analysis of Reading Difficulty* and the *Gates-McKillop Reading Diagnostic Test*.

2. *The use of the cloze test may be quite valuable in evaluating comprehension abilities of students.* (This test is explained in Chapter 2.)

By making a careful analysis of the answers that the student gives on the cloze test, one can make a decision relative to the reader's background and to whether or not he/she understands the meaning of words. This test also provides some information to the teacher relative to the learner's competency in the areas of context clues, vocabulary, and general meaning of various words.

3. *An informal comprehension test can be constructed by a teacher over any particular content area.*

After having decided the readability level of the content textbook, you can ask students to turn to a specific page in the book and read one to five pages silently. On a sheet of paper list five different comprehension questions and ask them to write the answers to the questions. These questions should represent all four levels of comprehension. Their responses should lend a fairly good impression regarding whether or not they can function at the various comprehension process levels.

4. *Study skills encompass many different types of competency.*

These might involve such things as organizing material, locating information, following directions, and using graphic aids of various sorts. Depending on the study skills stressed in your school for the learning level of your students, the best possible means of evaluating this important segment of skills is through an informal teacher-made test. For example, in the area of note taking, merely read a lecture that would be about ten minutes in length and have your students make an outline of the material that they heard. You could place on the overhead projector a transparency on which you have indicated what you feel is a model for note taking for that particular lecture. Have the students compare their notes with yours. The lecture could also be taped and the notes on the transparency uncovered as the material is presented on the tape.

If you want to check the students' ability to follow directions, simply read aloud four or five directions in a row and see if they can write them down in the order in which they were given. If you wish to evaluate their ability to locate information, utilize the textbook for the subject or content you are teaching and ask them a number of functional questions that would call for their using the various aspects of the book. One of the best ways of evaluating a student's ability to use maps, graphs, and charts is to show a map, graph, or chart on a bulletin board or overhead projector. Hand a list of questions to the students and ask them to answer each question using the graphic aid. Give the answers orally and let the students check to see whether or not they arrived at the right answer. If you desire the information for your own personal use, grade each of the papers individually.

5. *Oral questions that are asked of various students during a class discussion are a valuable way of finding
out whether or not individual students comprehend
certain kinds of information.*

Ask questions at the four different levels relating to a
unit of material and mentally assess the responses your students make to these kinds of questions. By carefully evaluating their responses, one can gain an impression whether they
have proficiency in coping with the various comprehension
skill tasks.

After using one or more of the diagnostic techniques
outlined above, collect all of the data from the various instruments and techniques and make a profile sheet for each student. The sheet would indicate the student's name and
whether or not the reader was proficient in the various comprehension and study skills. After determining which students need further help, use one or more of the procedures in
the next section for helping the students. These exercises are
classroom teacher-tested procedures that will help you immensely in preparing students for state and federally mandated competency examinations. They are useful for many
types of students.

FIFTEEN EFFECTIVE METHODS
FOR BUILDING COMPREHENSION SKILLS

There are many ways of helping students improve comprehension skills. The following are those that have been
most useful to the writer and dozens of successful teachers.
They are not listed in any particular order of priority or importance. You will need to select those that seem most appropriate for the learning level of your students.

1. *For helping readers develop skill in reading details, give
your students a copy of a short selection dealing with some
historical event.*

The article could, for example, be entitled, "When

Alabama and Oklahoma Became States." Approximately half of the essay could be devoted to the development of Oklahoma as a state and the other half relating to how Alabama came to be a state. At the end of the article, one could have three columns. The first column would deal with facts; the second column would have "Alabama" at the top; and "Oklahoma" would be at the top of the third column. In the facts column, list such phrases as, "When territory became a state," "Number of people during first census," "Chief crops of the territory," etc. The student is expected to supply the answers for each of the facts for each of the two states. This would be giving the student practice in locating details.

2. *To give students practice in locating main ideas, one might duplicate five short paragraphs on a piece of paper.*

At the bottom of the paper, list five main ideas in scrambled order. Ask the student to match the main idea with the paragraph on the same page. The key for the selection might be placed on the opposite side of the page to make the exercise self-corrective. Place copies of the exercise in a skills box along with all of the other lessons described in this section. If the sheets are laminated, they can be given to small groups of students or to individuals. If a grease pencil is used, these sheets can be used repeatedly.

3. *If some of your students have difficulty with sentence sequencing, you can use the following exercise very appropriately.*

List several sentences in which two things happen. Sometimes one thing happens after the other, and sometimes the two things happen at the same time. The student is directed to write a "1" over the part of the sentence that happens first and a "2" over the part that happens second, or last. For example, you may wish to write the sentence "Before Mother baked bread, she checked to see if she had the flour in the bin." The student would place a "1" over "checked to see if flour was in the bin," and a "2" over the first part of the sentence.

4. *To give practice in general sequencing, one can list several steps in the preparation of some product.*

For example, one may wish to list briefly the steps involved in making butter in a creamery. There might be as many as a dozen steps involved in the process. At the end of the selection, list eight different sentences representing the eight steps in the process of making butter. These would be in scrambled order and the student would be asked to renumber them so that they would correspond to the correct order of making butter.

5. *In giving practice in selecting the main idea, write several short paragraphs consisting of two or three sentences. Follow each paragraph with three multiple choice items representing possible main ideas for the paragraphs.*

The student is to identify the choice that is the best main idea for the paragraph he/she has just read. The key could be placed on the opposite side of the page for self-correction.

6. *Practice in using the context properly can be obtained by an interesting lesson sheet.*

Compose several short paragraphs of three or four sentences each. Leave out three or four key words in each of the paragraphs. Below each paragraph, list three words for each of the blanks. The student is directed to find the most plausible word for the blank in the paragraph. The key to the exercise could be supplied if desired. You may wish to show this exercise on a transparency and complete the exercise in a group setting so you can explain to your students why a given answer appears to be better than the other choices.

7. *For helping students build skills in the area of inferential comprehension, duplicate a short selection of 50-300 words, depending upon the age group you are teaching.*

Below the exercise, list four comprehension questions that are inferential in nature. This activity could be an individual or a classwide exercise. After the students have written the answers, have a class discussion regarding which answers are appropriate.

8. *In order to give practice in listening comprehension, read aloud a three or four paragraph selection involving a historical narrative.*

When you are through reading, ask the students to write the answers to specified questions. If desired, read the selection again and give the students a chance to change their answers if they desire.

9. *After having used one or more of the previous exercises, have your students read a given section in the content textbook.*

Ask each of them to write three or four comprehension questions that they think are reasonable and fair. Have them exchange questions with their classmates to determine if their peers can answer the questions. The writer and the respondent can have a short conference to discuss why certain answers are desired.

10. *After having studied the various propaganda techniques at the critical level of comprehension, place a tape recorder on the teacher's desk and invite the students to pretend that they are the advertising editor for your local paper. Ask them to compose a full page advertising copy for the recorder that will appear in next Sunday's edition.*

They should try to use as many propaganda techniques as possible. This exercise very often results in a good deal of good-natured humor among and between the classmates and the teacher.

11. *To practice securing the main idea, supply copies of a news article to your students and ask them to construct a suitable headline for the article just read.*

After they have indicated their own headline, compare it with the actual headline that appeared in the newspaper.

12. *In order to give your students practice in using graphic aids such as maps, graphs, and charts, find a chart or a map and enlarge it on the opaque or overhead projector.*

Ask your students specific questions such as "In what

year did Illinois have the most rainfall?" or "As a profession, which group makes the highest salary, dentists or doctors?" Demonstrate *why* certain responses are correct.

13. *To give students practice in summarizing and organizing, provide each student with a news story containing two to five paragraphs.*

Create a summary for the selection that contains both relevant and irrelevant sentences. Ask the students to underline the sentences that are relevant, and cross out any statements that are inappropriate. As an alternative, students could be asked to write their own summaries for the new articles.

14. *Predicting outcomes can be strengthened through the use of short selections.*

Supply your students with copies of a short story or narrative with the outcome of the story omitted. Ask them to write what they think the outcome was and compare it with the actual outcome printed in the original source. An alternative to this exercise would be supplying three or four outcomes and then letting the students select the one that they think is the proper one.

15. *One of the most ingenious exercises for developing awareness of the importance of following directions consists of a printed set of directions.*

Give a piece of paper to each student on which a number of directions have been printed. At the beginning of the page, write the sentence "Read all directions before starting this exercise." The second statement might read "Write your name at the lower left hand corner of the page." The third might be "Go to the front of the room and write on the board 'I am a good reader.'" Continue the page with the directions such as underlining the fourth word in the second sentence, etc. The last statement should be "Make no marks on this page. Give the page to your teacher." Those who did not follow directions will easily understand the motivation for the exercise.

The activities just described will be useful for several learning levels. The exact ones you will want to employ will be dependent upon the needs of your students. Select several and try them with your students. You will be delighted with the positive results.

PROCEDURES FOR DEVELOPING STUDY SKILLS

There are some students who appear to be able to pronounce and comprehend words at a very satisfactory level, but have a great deal of difficulty in reading assignments, taking notes, finding material in specialized sourcebooks, and summarizing information that has been obtained from several sources. Many of these same students have problems with studying various textbooks in preparation for a test. The purpose of this section is to provide several activities you can use to help students with this important skill segment. The number of activities selected will depend on the needs of the students you are instructing.

1. *If your students have not become acquainted with the SQ3R method, present lessons and exercises that will develop their proficiency in this important study technique.*

The SQ3R reading-study formula was developed by Francis P. Robinson of Ohio State in the mid-1940's. The steps of this technique are *survey, question, read, recite, and review.* There are numerous publications that have been written about this effective method. In the first step, *survey,* the student is to take note of the major features of the material to be read such as the headings, subheadings, and pictures in order to get a general idea of what the selection is about. The second step is *question* for gaining purposes for reading. The third stage is to actually *read* the material. The fourth stage, *recite,* is answering the questions posed in step two. The last stage, *review,* is trying to remember important things from the material at some later time. Using the actual material from your content textbook demonstrate to your students the

way this technique could be used with the text. On the overhead transparency, underline the topics, subtopics, and key
words to provide practice with this important procedure. To
ensure that they have developed these skills, hand the students duplicated copies of a related segment of content material and ask them to underline the key parts of the chapter,
write the questions, and perform other assignments that
would demonstrate that they understand this important technique.

2. *To give students practice in outlining, construct a sample
outline of one of the content textbooks the students use in
your class.*

Prepare an outline of the material and duplicate it so that
you can hand copies to your students. Have the same copy of
the material prepared on a transparency for use on the overhead projector. As your students look at their content
textbooks, point out various significant aspects of the outline
to them. At a later time, give students a partial outline of
another segment of the content textbook and ask them to
practice filling out the remainder of the outline. If time permits, it would be wise to examine each student's paper and
give pertinent suggestions as to how their outlines can be
improved.

3. *One of the greatest difficulties encountered by students is
studying for tests.*

Demonstrate the importance of looking for key words
that are underlined or italicized. They should look for important words in the subtopics of the material on which they are
being tested. Help them try to determine what questions
might be important to the teacher administering the test.
Demonstrate how to read test questions, such as true/false
and multiple choice items. Emphasize that test questions
must be read very carefully and that only the answer that is
requested should be placed on the sheet.

4. *There are a number of commercial materials available for
helping the student improve his/her study skills.*

Some of these materials are as follows:

Study Skills Program (Contemporary Books, Inc.)
Master Reading Program (Master Reading Ed. and Dev., Inc.)
Building Reading Skills (McDougal Littell and Company)
Reading and Study Skills (McGraw-Hill Book Company)

5. *Since some students have difficulty locating appropriate resource books for specific assignments, prepare simulated situations that require the student to use various resource books in the library such as the Reader's Guide, the World Almanac, and encyclopedias of different kinds.*

If possible, give different questions to different students in order to force them to work individually. These questions should be typical of the class or content area you are teaching.

Summary

Comprehension is one of the most complex aspects of the total reading act. It does not consist of a single skill, but rather is global in nature and includes at least four levels: literal, interpretative, critical, and creative. There are a number of factors involved in comprehension abilities, such as physical and emotional development, intelligence, background, and word attack ability. There are a number of teacher-tested activities you can employ for building both comprehension and study skills. For effective correction of comprehension deficiencies, one needs to conduct a careful diagnosis of each student's competency in this important area and build a prescriptive program that fits his/her needs.

REFERENCES

1. Bond, Guy L., Tinker, Miles A., and Wasson, Barbara B. *Reading Difficulties, Their Diagnosis and Correction.* Englewood Cliffs, N. J.: Prentice-Hall, Inc., 1979. Ch. 13.

2. Cushenbery, Donald C. *Reading Improvement Through Diagnosis, Remediation, and Individualized Instruction.* West Nyack, N. Y.: Parker Publishing Company, Inc., 1977. Ch. 6.

3. Goodman, Kenneth S., "A Linguistic Study of Cues and Miscues in Reading," *Elementary English*, 42, (October, 1965) pp. 639-643.

4. McNeil, John D., Donant, Lizbeth and Alkin, Marvin C. *How To Teach Reading Successfully.* Boston: Little, Brown and Company, 1980. Ch. 5.

5. Shepherd, David L. *Comprehensive High School Reading Methods.* Columbus: Charles E. Merrill Publishing Company, 1978. Ch. 4.

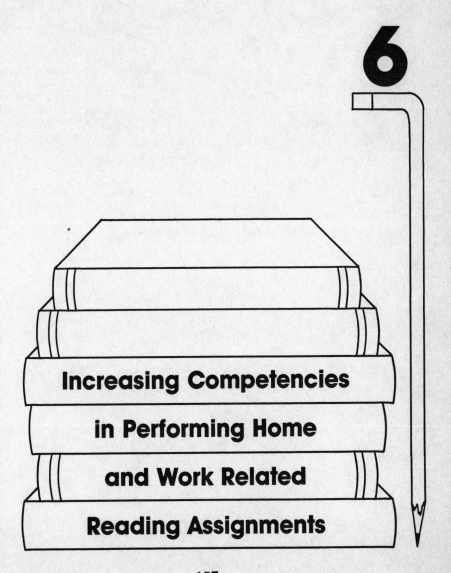

Increasing Competencies in Performing Home and Work Related Reading Assignments

6

The information in the previous five chapters has dealt with many important aspects of diagnostic and corrective instruction. Important information has been given relative to teacher-tested approaches to building vocabulary, word analysis, comprehension, and study skills. All of these skills are very important to active reading in the various content areas during the regular school day.

The worth of a given reading program, however, can only be determined by how well a student performs in home and work related reading assignments. While many of the state-mandated competency tests emphasize such skills as application forms, recipes, advertisements and similar types of materials, the student also has need for these types of skills on a day-to-day basis. Therefore, if a student in your school is to perform effectively in out-of-school experiences, he/she must be competent in these types of reading tasks. In other words, the learner must make the connection between skills required in classroom assignments and those that are needed to perform work related reading assignments. The general public will have a favorable opinion of the school reading program only when that program produces skilled readers who can read contracts, write letters of application, and complete loan and apartment application forms.

Accordingly, your reading program should emphasize many types of skill development that a given student will use on a daily basis. To supply important information with respect to how to work with your students in this important area, the following topics are included in this chapter: (1) the nature of home and work related reading assignments; (2) evaluating skill development in home and work related reading assignments; and (3) 20 classroom tested techniques for building home and work related reading skills. At the close of the chapter is a summary of the information along with a selected list of references relating to this important topic.

HOME AND WORK RELATED READING ASSIGNMENTS

Once a young person leaves high school, he/she finds that there are many opportunities and demands for performing various reading tasks. Depending on the occupation a given learner pursues, one may find as few as three or four general tasks required or as many as 35 or 50 tasks of a reading nature that are demanded in other professions. Regardless of one's profession or occupation, there are a number of reading tasks common to most people. The following is a sample of some of these tasks.

1. Shopping the grocery ads and understanding the prices and where various food items might be cheaper in a given city.
2. Reading the labels on cans, boxes and other related store items.
3. Reading and obeying street and highways signs.
4. Reading maps of various types to decide the number of miles involved between two cities.
5. Understanding and using a telephone directory.
6. Reading and obeying the directions given on a prescription medicine label.
7. Using and understanding how to purchase an item from a store catalog such as those published by Sears Roebuck, Montgomery Ward, and J. C. Penney.

8. Finding information from an index in a book, magazine, or in the yellow pages of the telephone directory.

9. Comprehending details of classified ads in the newspaper such as those dealing with what, where, when, and why.

10. Understanding the implications from drawings of floor plans and other similar designs.

11. Reading, understanding, and supplying the correct information on a job application form.

12. Completing correctly a loan and/or apartment application form.

13. Reading and understanding restaurant menus with respect to items offered, prices for each of the items, and other relevant information.

14. Comprehending various tables, such as those dealing with postal rates, mileage, bus and airplane schedules, as well as athletic schedules.

15. Reading and comprehending the detailed provisions of installment contracts, policies and similar documents that might be supplied by an employer regarding such practices as health insurance, sick leave, and other types of information.

16. Organizing and writing a letter of application for a desired position.

17. Utilizing special sources in a school or public library such as the Reader's Guide or the World Almanac.

18. Reading and comprehending a driver's license manual and the license examination.

The above is a mere sampling of the home and work related reading assignments that most young people are expected to complete. The motivation for developing these skills comes from a number of different sources such as personal satisfaction, securing a desired job, receiving a driver's license, or moving into a new apartment. In some instances the ability or inability to perform these functions may result in an emergency situation for a given individual. If, for example, he/she cannot read and understand bus and plane schedules, the individual may be late to a given appointment, or not secure an important job because the application was not submitted by the deadline. Some young people are of the opinion that they can depend on others for reading and delivering different types of information to them. They need to be impressed with the fact that, in many instances, they are alone and have to secure information in a hurry and cannot depend on another person to read and comprehend different kinds of information.

One of the important aspects of any school reading program, particularly at the secondary level, is providing each student with a firm foundation in reading with respect to vocabulary, word attack and comprehension. It should also supply every student with the skills necessary to perform the reading tasks demanded by the daily activities at home and work. In fact, a number of citizens in a given community will judge the value of the school reading program on the basis of how well their graduates are able to perform these kinds of tasks. It is necessary for every teacher of reading to evaluate the individual skill levels of each student in the home and work related reading skill areas. A profile sheet should be constructed for students listing the student's name on the left side of the page and the skills that should be accomplished at the top of the page. The sampling of 18 different skills indicated earlier in this chapter might be a starting place. The levels of skill development, of course, should be evaluated by some of the techniques indicated in the next section. If a student is found to be somewhat limited in these tasks, several of the classroom tested techniques that are noted in the third section of this chapter should be employed with the student in question. There are also a number of commercial materials, recently published and distributed, that can be quite helpful for students who need help with these types of reading skills. You can find the names of these materials along with their respective publishers in the appendices section of this volume. Since there is a great deal of emphasis in local and state mandated reading tests on work-related reading assignments, there are many publishers who are active in producing these kinds of materials at the present time.

EVALUATING SKILL DEVELOPMENT
IN HOME AND WORK RELATED READING ASSIGNMENTS

There are few, if any, commercial and/or standardized tests available for measuring these important skills. The best way to conduct an effective program of evaluation is simply to take the actual documents that demand reading proficiency and use those in a diagnostic setting. If you wish to evaluate a total class or a large group, many stores and agencies will be happy to supply enough copies of catalogs, application forms, and other similar pieces of information for undertaking your diagnostic program.

There are several aspects to keep in mind when devising a program of analysis of skill development in home and work related reading assignments. First of all, decide what skills you desire your students to acquire. Second, compose a relevant task that involves the skills you have decided are important. Third, determine the level of proficiency you demand for each of the evaluative tests or exercises you are going to ask each student to undertake. Fourth, proceed with different kinds of techniques for helping students who need further practice in these kinds of skills. In the next section of this chapter you will find 20 classroom-tested techniques for building these skills.

As has been the case with the other skill areas described in this volume, one should develop a profile sheet to indicate several pieces of important information. This sheet can be in the form of a grid with the names of the students listed on the left side of the sheet, and the names of all of the various skills that you are emphasizing at the top of the sheet. After analyzing the results on the diagnostic instruments, place an "X" in the skill area for the student who scores below the critical level you have predetermined to be satisfactory for that skill. A careful study of the profile sheet will give an excellent picture of the types of teaching strategies you should undertake for helping individual students and those in small and larger groups. The skills you should assess and promote quite obviously are those in which you are convinced your students will need proficiency as they enter the work market. An additional consideration would be those emphasized on the competency tests administered to your students by local or state authorities. One of the problems with many reluctant readers in every area of skill development is that of lack of motivation for pursuing various reading goals. The information in the next chapter will give much practical help in working with students who have problems with motivation. If you use the proper materials for evaluation, as well as for teaching, and demonstrate to the students the need for developing skills in the various strategic areas, you will help them to be successful in the occupation they will pursue at some later time.

Diagnostic Procedures for Evaluating Home and Work Related Reading Assignments

Since there is a scarcity of standardized and commercial tests for any type of formal assessment of the myriad skills in this important area, one must devise a number of teacher-directed informal techniques for diagnosis. The following is a list of practical suggestions that have been used by many successful teachers for accomplishing this important goal. The list involves the evaluating process for the various skills enumerated earlier in this chapter. The order of the evaluative techniques is in the same order as the skills were listed. It is suggested that for each of the following suggestions, you list at least five different questions or directions. A critical level of 80 percent proficiency might be established. This means that the student would need to complete at least four out of five directions or questions for a given skill.

1. *Shopping the Grocery Ads*

Make copies of four different grocery ads that advertise several common products for sale. For example, find those that are featuring Kellogg's Corn Flakes and Van Camp's Pork and Beans and other products. Copies of these ads can be laminated or duplicated (with permission of the stores). The following would be five questions you could ask about the four ads:

    a. Which store has the lowest price for the 13-oz. box of Kellogg's Corn Flakes?

    b. If you needed to buy a 50-pound sack of potatoes, 2 cans of Van Camp's Pork and Beans, and 1 jar of Heinz pickles, at which store could you buy these three items for the lowest price?

    c. At Johnson's Market, what would be the price of 2 cans of DelMonte Sweet Peas, 1 can of Alpo dogfood, and 2 pounds of Thompson Seedless Grapes?

    d. If you would buy 5 cans of Surefine Green Beans at the Safeway supermarket and gave the checkout person a $10 bill, how much change should you receive? (The sales tax for the 5 cans is 7 cents).

    e. Is the following statement true or false? You would have to have at least $1 to buy a box of Baker's Coconut at *any* of the stores.

2. *Reading Labels on Cans and Boxes*

Remove the labels from three cans of food and cut the front from two boxes of cereal or other related products. This material could be duplicated and laminated according to your desire. List five statements on a piece of paper and ask the student to write "yes" or "no" in front of each statement if the information contained in the statement can be found on any of the labels. The following are examples.

    a. The can of green beans contains at least five servings.

    b. The can of beans contains 5 ounces of food.

c. The box of cornflakes is produced by the Kellogg Company, Battle Creek, Michigan.

d. The contents of the box of scalloped potatoes must be mixed with hot water and butter and then baked in the oven.

e. One of the ingredients in the can of mushrooms is salt.

3. *Reading and Obeying Street and Highway Signs*

Cut pictures of road signs from old driver's license manuals and duplicate them on a sheet of paper. Compile five true/false items concerning the information found on the signs. You may wish to use some of the sample questions that are provided in many of the driver's license manuals for the various states.

4. *Reading Maps to Find Distances*

Ask the Chamber of Commerce officer in your city to supply enough copies of city maps for all of your students. Compile five different test items in which the student must choose the correct word and write it on the blank in the statement. The following are five examples of statements you could use for the map exercise.

a. The police station is located on _____ Street.

b. Highway 265 is approximately _____ miles north of Elm Street.

c. 65th Street is _____ blocks north of the expressway.

d. The State fairgrounds is in the _____ part of the city.

e. Northwestern University is located on _____ Street.

5. *Understanding and Using a Telephone Directory*

For this exercise you may wish to use old telephone directories that have been discarded by offices or the telephone company. Large businesses quite frequently will give their old telephone directories to schools for teaching purposes. Be sure each of your students has the same directory. To evaluate a student's ability in using this source, merely list

five statements that call for very specific information. The
following are examples.

   a. What is the area code for Ann Arbor, Michigan?

   b. What is the number you would dial if you wish to reach
      the police department?

   c. On what page of the directory would you find the tele-
      phone number for Donald L. Chapman?

   d. Look in the Yellow Pages and find the section that
      lists "Movers." What moving company has the tele-
      phone number of 334-2245?

   e. What phone number would you dial if you wanted re-
      pair service on your telephone?

6. *Reading and Obeying Directions on Prescription
    Labels*

To evaluate a student's ability in this area, secure several
prescription labels from a local drugstore and type various
directions on labels. You could xerox these labels on a piece of
paper and then indicate five statements below the labels that
each student would be asked to mark either "true" or "false."

7. *Using Store Catalogs*

Some companies provide old store catalogs for use by schools
in teaching purposes. If this is not possible, some of the major
nation-wide stores such as Sears and Penneys sell catalogs for
$2 each. In any case, be sure that each student has a common
catalog for the evaluative exercise. The five examples you
compile may involve true/false statements, multiple-choice
items, or blanks that call for specific information. These items
could demand that the student figure prices for a number of
items, calculate postage, and determine if he/she has enough
money to buy a certain number of items.

8. *Finding Information From an Index*

Very often a person is required to find information in a book
or magazine in minimal time. One could cut the index sections

from a number of old books or magazines, laminate them, and use them on an individual basis with a number of students. Compile questions or directions for each of the indexes used for the exercise. You could use true/false statements for the evaluative purpose.

9. *Comprehending Details of Classified Ads in a News-paper*

Most citizens read a daily newspaper, and many people look at the classified ads to find a job, buy a product, or find other kinds of information. Most daily newspapers will supply 20 or 30 copies of any one day's paper for a teacher undertaking exercises that deal with the appropriate use of newspapers. After distributing the newspapers, ask each student to turn to the classified section to answer five questions. The following are examples:

a. What is the price of a new Pinto Marwell Ford?

b. What is the number of the classified section that deals with "Personals"?

c. Write the name of at least one employment agency that advertised in the classified section.

d. If you wanted to sell some used furniture, what is the number of the section where you would advertise?

e. Look in the section entitled, "Automobiles for Sale." Write the name of one of the automobile dealers that sell new Pontiac Firebirds.

10. *Understanding the Implication of Drawings of Floor Plans*

From time to time, persons are shown drawings of floor plans or similar documents and need to understand the implications of these drawings as they prepare to paint, redecorate, re-model, etc. For the evaluation of this particular skill, one might show a sample set of floor plans of the classroom where the students are being taught. Five completion statements could be compiled that would call for each student's understanding of the length and width of the room, the width of the windows, distance from the window to the floor, how wide the door is, etc.

11. *Applying for a Job*

Practically all of your students will apply for a job at some time and it is necessary that they understand how to fill out a job application form appropriately. One of the best ways of evaluating this skill is to get as many job application forms as needed from a local employer. Compile five multiple-choice questions concerning the application form you have supplied. The following might be samples of such questions:

a. A good answer for line 4 would be (1) 20; (2) 562-7120; (3) 512-24-7512; (4) 9-24-80.

b. If you cannot use one of your arms, where would you write this information?: 1) line 8; (2) line 9; (3) line 4; (4) line 1.

Proceed to make three more such statements. The student should be able to answer four out of five if he/she has adequate proficiency in understanding and completing a job application form.

12. *Completing Loan and Apartment Application Forms*

These kinds of forms are very common to most people, and it is imperative that your students understand how to complete such forms efficiently and effectively. You could evaluate each student's competency in this important skill by using the exact loan or apartment application forms secured from local businesses. For evaluating this important skill, ask each student to complete these forms. After they have completed the forms see if they have completed them with at least 80-90 percent accuracy on all of the blanks on the forms.

13. *Reading and Understanding Restaurant Menus*

There are literally hundreds of different types of restaurants in this country. Moreover, the items offered, their prices, and the amount of gratuity are somewhat puzzling to many people.

To evaluate this important skill, one might use actual restaurant menus supplied by a local business. Supply each student with a list of five true/false statements and ask each of them to study the menu and determine whether or not each statement is "true" or "false." The following might be examples of such statements:

a. The price of Beef Wellington is less than that of Rib Eye steak.

b. If one had $10, one could pay for a T-bone steak, a glass of iced tea, and the cherry pie alamode.

c. Steaks can only be ordered after 7 p.m. in this restaurant.

d. Large colas cost 75 cents.

e. The soup of the day is Cream of Mushroom.

14. *Comprehending Postal Rate, Mileage, Bus Schedules and Other Types of Charts*

During one's lifetime there are many times when an individual needs to read and understand charts of this type. The evaluation of this skill can be undertaken in a fairly simple fashion by collecting these types of documents from businesses such as bus stations, airline terminals, and a local United States Post Office. In the case of an airplane schedule, one might supply each student with a common plane schedule (such as United or American Airlines) and ask five statements calling for very detailed answers. The student should supply the information for at least four of the five statements. The following are examples of such completion statements:

a. What is the earliest time of day that one can depart Des Moines for Omaha?

b. Is it possible to go from Chicago to Memphis in the morning and return from Memphis to Chicago the same day?

c. At what time of the day does American Airlines Flight #262 leave Denver for Los Angeles?

d. Does it take longer to fly from Dallas to New York, or from Chicago to Los Angeles?

e. Is it possible to leave Kansas City for Chicago between 8 a.m. and 10 a.m. on any given day?

15. *Determining Provisions of Installment Contracts, Policies and Other Similar Documents*

Nearly every person buys some kind of product during a lifetime on an installment contract. Unfortunately, many people don't understand the details of installment contracts and frequently find themselves in financial difficulties. It is imperative that your students develop this skill for later life and for any questions regarding this type of skill on competency examinations. Many stores will provide sample installment contracts for your use in the diagnosis and teaching of this particular skill. Probably the best way to evaluate each student's competency is to have all students fill out one of the contracts and determine if they are able to complete at least 80 percent of the requested information in an effective manner. Those students who make errors should be informed of their errors and helped to see what they could do to improve their skill in this area.

16. *Compiling, Writing, and Organizing a Letter of Application*

Of all the skills mentioned thus far, the skill of writing a correct letter of application is probably one of the most neglected. Many young people fail to secure employment because they have misspelled words, have not included the correct information, and have committed other types of errors. One of the best ways to evaluate a student's skill in this particular aspect of work related competencies is to duplicate a sample letter of application on which there are five different errors. These errors could consist of misspelled words, incorrect address for the employer, and other related types of errors. The student is to recopy the letter error-free. Those students who can detect at least four of the five errors and eliminate them in his/her final copy of the letter should be considered efficient in this skill.

17. *Utilizing Special Sources in a School or Public Library*

Many of your students will make use of the public library after they have left your school in order to find job-related information. If they are to find the information in a suitable way, they will, of course, need to use specialized sources such as the Reader's Guide, World Almanac, and different types of encyclopedias. To evaluate this skill, one could list five questions calling for the students to use these specialized sources. This could be a matching type of exercise in which one side of the page would list the specialized sources, and the other side would have a list of different types of questions. The students would need to match the question with the appropriate source where the information could be found.

18. *Reading and Comprehending a Driver's License Examination*

One of the most pertinent motivating forces for reading for any youth is the study of a driver's license examination study booklet. Most young people want to drive a car and this skill is absolutely vital if they are to meet the goals of securing a driver's license. To evaluate this skill, one could secure several state driver's license examination study booklets. If the booklets don't contain sample questions or study questions, you could compile five questions that would demand different types of information. The following are samples of the types of questions you might ask each student:

a. What is the legal speed limit for the residential streets of the city?

b. Do you have to come to a stop when you see a yield sign?

c. How should you signal with your hand if you want to make a right turn?

d. You must park at least how many feet from a fire hydrant?

e. How often must you renew your driver's license in this state?

As indicated in the previous section, there are numerous ways of evaluating home and work related reading assignments. Since there are few, if any, standardized or commercial tests available for this type of reading skill, you will need to compile evaluative tests of your own to suit the precise needs of your students. The suggestions provided should give you some practical ideas for fulfilling this type of instructional task.

Those students identified as being limited in the 18 skill areas described in this chapter will need some additional practice to help them develop a desired level of competency for their own uses as well as for local and state mandated reading tests. In the next section, there are some suggestions you may wish to follow for accomplishing this instructional goal. There are many commercial materials available at the present time for helping students in these important areas and they are mentioned in the next section as well as in the appendices.

TWENTY CLASSROOM TESTED TECHNIQUES FOR BUILDING HOME AND WORK RELATED READING SKILLS

After utilizing many of the evaluative procedures described in the previous section, it would be appropriate to build a profile sheet indicating each student's name and his/ her areas of strengths and limitations in the 18 skill areas described previously. Other skills should be added that correlate closely with those emphasized on competency tests and/or demanded in work experiences common to *your* students.

A careful inspection of the profile sheet should provide valuable data and insight relative to the exact instructional needs of any given student. The techniques and strategies employed with any reader should be governed by the following principles:

A. The assigned lesson is appropriate for a learner when preferred learning modalities and demonstrated limitations are considered.

B. Informal as well as commercial hardware and software materials should be utilized.

C. A program of continuous evaluation of the skill development of each student should be in evidence to help insure that strategies are valid and useful.

D. Each student's program should be individualized as much as possible. (There is a temptation to ask all students to complete all assignments in a given commercial material. Obviously, not all exercises are needed for all students).

Many of the suggestions enumerated in the previous section as possible diagnostic strategies can also be used for skill development. In addition, the following section contains a description of 20 classroom tested techniques that may be employed in a number of teaching/learning siutations. They are not listed in any particular order of importance. The activities you select may need to be altered to meet individual requirements.

Activities A through J consist of sample forms and other pieces of data that provide meaningful practice for your students in a number of different home and work situations.

Activities K through R comprise descriptions of practical strategies that can be undertaken with selected students. There are a number of commercial materials available for building these important skills. The description and source of these aids can be found in Appendix A.

A. SCHOOL ENROLLMENT FORM

> **CENTERVIEW PUBLIC SCHOOLS—ENROLLMENT FORM**
> Centerview, Kentucky 28142
> Name *Mark Brown*   Address *6720 Ohio*
> Effective date of enrollment *Jan. 3, 1981* Age *14* Grade *9*
> Counselor's Name *M. Ball*   Office Number *162*
> Locker number *22* Home Room Teacher *Mrs. Lewis*
> First period subject *Art*   Second period subject *Biology*
> Third period subject *Algebra* Fourth period subject *P.E.*
> Fifth period subject *History*   Sixth period subject *Physics*
> **COMPLETE THIS FORM AND HAND IT TO YOUR COUNSELOR**

Directions:

Study the completed form above and answer each of the five questions with a "yes" or "no". If the information is not given, write the words, "Not given."

1. Mark's counselor and home room teacher are the same person. _____
2. Mark plays in the school band. _____
3. His Biology class is probably in the morning. _____
4. His locker number is 22. _____
5. Mark should take this completed form and give it to Mrs. Lewis. _____

B. CREDIT APPLICATION FORM

> **PLEASANT VALLEY DISCOUNT STORE — CREDIT APPLICATION**
> 1. _____
> (Please print) First Name Middle Name   Last Name
> 2. _____
> Address: Street   City   State   Zip Code

3. _____

Social Security No.   Phone No.   Present Employer

4. _____

Salary: Monthly   Weekly   Yearly

5. How long have you lived in this city at the above address?

_____

6. May we check your credit status at the Allen County Credit Bureau?   yes __   no __

7. List the names and addresses of four credit references (not relatives):

Directions:

Underline the best answer for each of the following items.

1. If you gave permission to have your credit checked, you should put this information on (a) line 6; (b) line 3; (c) line 7; (d) line 5.

2. Line 4 requires information about the applicant's (a) age; (b) salary; (c) name.

3. "2821 Ontario Avenue" would be a good answer for line (a) 5; (b) 6; (c) 2; (d) 3.

4. Lines 1 and 2 on the application provide information relating to (a) the applicant's name and address; (b) how much money the applicant makes; (c) the applicant's credit references; (d) none of the previous.

5. "$400.00" would be the best answer for line number (a) 7; (b) 4; (c) 5; (d) 1

C. LOAN APPLICATION FORM

WATERLOO VALLEY LOAN CORPORATION — LOAN APPLICATION

1. Name(s) of applicant(s) _____
2. Address of applicant(s) _____
3. Phone No. _____ 4. Social Security No. _____
   Applicant's present occupation _____
6. If married, spouse's occupation _____
7. List last two locations or places of employment with salary
   Placement of Employment   Year   Yearly   Salary

   _____   _____   _____

   _____   _____   _____

8. List outstanding loans (and amounts) which you have at present with other companies and businesses.

   _____

   _____

9. List purpose of loan.

   _____

   _____

Directions:

Select the *best* answer for each item.

1. You live at 1902 Elm Street. On what line would you place this information? (a) on line 2; (b) on line 1; (c) on line 3; (d) on line 8.

2. You owe Myers Drug a total of $200.00. Where does this information go? (a) on line 9; (b) on line 2; (c) on line 8; (d) on line 3.

3. You plan to go on a trip. Where would you place this fact? (a) on line 2; (b) there is no line for this; (c) on line 3; (d) on line 4.

4. You would place your phone number on (a) line 4; (b) line 3; (c) line 2; (d) line 8.

5. Your name should go on (a) line 2; (b) line 1; (c) line 3; (d) line 8.

D. BASEBALL STANDINGS

MAJOR LEAGUE STANDINGS

AMERICAN LEAGUE					NATIONAL LEAGUE				
EAST					EAST				
	W	L	Pct.	GB		W	L	Pct.	GB
Detroit	85	51	.624	-	St. Louis	74	63	.540	-
Boston	80	55	.593	4½	Pittsburgh	72	63	.533	1
Baltimore	73	60	.549	10½	Philadelphia	72	65	.526	2
New York	71	64	.526	13½	Montreal	61	74	.452	12
Milwaukee	73	66	.525	13½	New York	59	78	.431	15
Cleveland	70	65	.519	14½	Chicago	53	82	.393	20
Toronto	58	78	.416	27					
WEST					WEST				
Minnesota	87	50	.635	-	Atlanta	79	58	.577	-
Oakland	68	68	.500	18½	Cincinnati	77	60	.562	2
Texas	68	70	.493	19½	Houston	74	63	.540	5
Kansas City	60	79	.432	28	Los Angeles	71	65	.522	7½
Chicago	57	78	.422	29	San				
California	52	82	.388	33½	Francisco	67	70	.489	12
Seattle	50	86	.368	36½	San Diego	60	78	.435	19½

Directions:

Read the above standings very carefully. For each of the following statements write *yes* if the statement is true. Write *no* if the statement is *false*.

1. Cleveland has won more games than St. Louis. _____
2. There is some chance that Minnesota will win the World Series. _____
3. Oakland is 18½ games behind Kansas City. _____
4. Atlanta is the leader in the American League West Division. _____
5. Houston and Boston have both won the same number of games. _____

E. TELEVISION SCHEDULE

Midlands TV

SARZ-NBC	Channel 1
MOTZ-CBS	Channel 2
TORI-ABC	Channel 3
SURI-TV	Channel 4
MOS-TV	Channel 5
TOT-TV	Channel 6

Listings are supplied by the stations

FRIDAY NIGHT

5:00 p.m.

1 Evening News
2 Nightly News
3 Midlands News
4 Jack's Jungle
5 Mr. Atom
6 McDaniel Speaks

5:30 p.m.

1 NBC Nightly News
2 CBS Evening News
3 World News Tonight
4 Jack's Jungle
5 Money Talks
6 McDaniel Speaks

6:00 p.m.

1 Music For You
2 Play for Money
3 Local Sports
4 Concert Shorts
5 Farm Topics
6 Sign Off

6:30 p.m.

1 NBC Special
2 Teacher Talks
3 Our City
4 Oral Roberts
5 You Can Speak

7:00 p.m.

1 UNO Profile
2 Mayor James
3 Movie of The Week
4 Today's Pastor
5 Ask a Question

7:30 p.m.

1 UNO Profile
2 Mayor James
3 Movie of The Week
4 Election Week
5 How Do You Do It?

8:00 p.m.

1   Movie (to 10 p.m.)
2   Eden North
3   Madison Avenue play
4   Mr. Smith
5   Money from Oscar

10:00 p.m.

1   News at 10
2   Late News
3   News 3
4   Ray Ewing Hour
5   Your News

9:00 p.m.

1   Movie
2   Football
3   Madison Avenue play
4   Your Question
5   Health topics

Directions:

Read the schedule carefully. Find the right answers for the blanks in the statements.

1. Mayor James speaks on Channel 2 at ____ p.m.

2. Teacher Talks is aired on Channel ____ at ____ p.m.

3. The movie on Channel 1 lasts for ____ minutes.

4. If you wish to tune in for Today's Pastor, you should select Channel ____ at ____ p.m.

5. Between 5:00 p.m. and 10:30 p.m. Channel 2 has ____ newscasts.

F. USING INDEXES (PART 1)

Index from *Grover City Telegram*	
Classified Ads 5B	Obituaries.....................3B
Financial 4B	Your Point of View 1B
Editorials 8A	TV schedules 6A
Sports 7A	Weather 2B

Index from *Starland Daily Dispatch*	
Bridge 15	Editorial 23
Classified 18-20	Features 24-25
Comics 21	Jonesy 27
Crossword 22	Horoscope 27

Movies 27	Stock Market...................31
Pictures 28	TV log.............................32
Sports 29-30	

Directions:

Look at the two indexes above. Write the correct answer on the blanks below.

1. In which paper will your find your horoscope?

   _____

2. Which newspaper has crossword puzzles?

   _____

3. On what pages do you find the classified ads in the *Starland Daily Dispatch*? _____

4. Which paper does not list the obituaries?

   _____

5. Which paper has a feature called "Jonesy"?

   _____

G. USING INDEXES (PART 2)

A

Ability group, 22
Academic Promise Tests, 130
Ames, Wilbur S. 19, 30, 232
Artley, A. Sterl, 62, 86, 191
Ashlock, Patrick, 227
Audio-visual materials and devices, 213-217

B

Bamman, Henry A., 98, 142, 154, 173
Berkey, Sally C., 179, 191
Berkley, U. Ellis, 179, 191
Berry, Althea, 46
Binet Intelligence Test, 40
Blends, 51
Bond, Guy L., 32, 36, 38, 46, 86, 120, 139, 183, 227

Bond expectancy formula, 32, 33
Book clubs for youth, 153, 225
Book reports, 152
Book series, 195
Botel, Morton, 62
Botel Reading Inventory, 127
Brown, Earl, 189
Brown-Carlsen Listening Comprehension Test, 84, 130
Broz, James Jr., 228
Burns, Paul C., 30, 62, 140
Buros, Oscar Krisen, 131, 228

C

California Phonics Survey, 127

California Reading Tests, 84, 127	following directions, 72
California Test of Personality, 130	noting the author's plan, 74
Carlson, G. Robert, 228	reading critically, 78-81
Carter, Homer L., 228	reading for detail, 69
Chall, Jeanne S., 139	reading maps, graphs, and charts, 76
Chase, Naomi C., 98	skill strands, 68
Cloze procedure, 134	summarizing and organizing, 77
Cohn, Jack, 228	Comprehension Tests of Basic Skills, 84
Cohn, Stella M., 228	Content area reading:
Comprehension:	difficulty in texts, 102-104
developmental materials, 85	in industrial arts, 115-117
evaluation, 83, 84	in language arts, 104-106
Comprehension skill:	in mathematics, 117-119
finding the main idea, 70	in science, 106-109
following a sequence of events, 71	

Directions:

Above is part of an index from a library book. Study it carefully and read the five statements below. If the statement is true, write "yes" on the blank at the end of the sentence. If it is false, write "no".

1. There is information in this book concerning the *Boatright Phonics Test.* ____

2. The cloze procedure is described on page 134. ____

3. There is only one place in this book which contains information on the *Botel Reading Inventory.* ____

4. James Bectel is quoted on page 28. ____

5. Comprehension skill strands are discussed on page 68. ____

H. UNDERSTANDING GRAPHS

Total Enrollment in Elmwood High School

320	620	800	825	847	860	762
1974	1975	1976	1977	1978	1979	1980

Directions:

Study the graph above and complete the blanks with the right answers.

1. This graph shows information for ____ years.
2. In 1978, ____ were enrolled.
3. The largest enrollment was in ____.
4. From 1979 to 1980 the enrollment dropped by ____.
5. In which year were 825 enrolled? ____

I. RESTAURANT MENU

Joe's Midtown Cafe

1. STEAKBURGER SPECIAL
   Steakburger, French fries, and tossed salad.....$2.69
2. CHICKEN SPECIAL
   Fried chicken, French fries, cole slaw $2.89
3. CHEESEBURGER SPECIAL
   Cheeseburger, French fries, baked beans.........$3.00
4. FISH SPECIAL
   Catfish, coleslaw, baked beans $3.00

Sandwich Menu   SIDE ORDERS
1. STEAKBURGER ....$1.80 FRENCH FRIED ONION
   Large ....$2.50   RINGS $1.50

2. CHEESEBURGER $2.00
     Large $2.60
3. HAMBURGER DELUXE
   (with lettuce, tomato,
   salad dressing)............$1.75
4. BAKED HAM $1.90
5. BACON, LETTUCE,
   TOMATO $2.20
6. GRILLED CHEESE...$1.80
7. TUNA SALAD...........$2.00

BAKED POTATO
(after 7:00
  p.m. only) $1.25
FRENCH FRIED
  POTATOES ....$ .90
SOUP OF THE DAY
  (bowl) $1.50

SALADS
COLE SLAW.............$ .80
TOSSED SALAD........$ .95
TOMATO ....$ .85
POTATO ....$ .95
SWEET CORN..........$1.10

Directions:
   Study the menu above. Write the correct answers on the
blanks in the sentences below.

   1. The cost of a baked ham sandwich and an order of
      cole slaw is $____.
   2. The price of the steakburger special is $2.69. If you
      ordered the steakburger, French fries, and tossed
      salad separately, how much would the total be? ____
   3. Which is cheaper, a grilled cheese sandwich or a
      cheeseburger? _____
   4. Could you have a baked potato at noon? (yes or no)
      ____
   5. The hamburger deluxe contains _____,
      _____ and _____.

J. PRESCRIPTION LABELS

GETTUMWELL PRESCRIPTIONS 2260 Freedright Avenue Cottonwood, Oklahoma 83145	MARVEL VALLEY DRUG STORE 1156 West Cadillack Drive Moose Valley, Nebraska 68199
------------------- 9-9-80 Patient: W. A. McClintocks Directions: Two tablets after meals and at bedtime as needed. RX 45316 alginic acid Dr. Murray A. Hartenet	-------------------- 9-9-80 Patient: Howard L. McCulluz Directions: Chew 1 or 2 tablets every 2 to 4 hours as needed. RX 22341 Magnesium Trisilicate Dr. Holley W. Brown

Directions:

Study the two prescription labels above. Fill in the blanks in the following sentences with the correct answer.

1. Mr. McCulluz' doctor is _____.

2. He should take ____ alginic acid tablets after meals and bedtime as needed.

3. The name of the drug prescribed by Dr. Brown was

    _____.

4. He should not take more than ____ alginic acid tablets in 24 hours.

5. The prescription number for Mr. McClintock's drug is

    _____.

K.

To give practice in comprehending and interpreting information found on cans and boxes, cut pertinent sections from cereal boxes, vegetable cans, etc. which contain data relating to such items as ingredients and directions for cooking. Laminate these items and place in files with tabs for proper identification of materials. On the back of each item laminate several true/false, multiple-choice, or completion statements for the student to complete. Answers for each set of statements can be included. All of the files and answers could be placed in one box for easy storage and use.

L.

Skill in using a store catalogue in a proper manner can be realized by supplying each student with a copy of a catalogue obtained from a large store such as Wards, Sears, Penney's or Aldens. (Sometimes old catalogues are available. Unless one is a regular customer, new catalogues usually cost $2.00 or more each). The following are types of activities which can be used.

1. Complete an order form for four specified items.
2. Find the cost and postage involved for one particular article.
3. Find the page numbers where information is given about several items.
4. Examine catalogues from two companies. Compare the costs of similar items from the two sources.

M.

The prospect of receiving a valid state driver's license is effective motivation for most young people to read and comprehend significant concepts and facts relating to the driver's license test. To develop skill in this important area, one could clip several pages from a current driver's license manual and place each page in a separate file folder. Enclose a sheet which contains a number of sample test items involving the material found in the file. Place the key to the test items in a separate file. All files could be housed in a wooden or cardboard box. After students have read all of the information and completed all of the test items in the total box, they should be well prepared for the official license examination.

N.

Most people are obliged to read and sign financial contracts of various types during the course of a lifetime. These contracts and agreements involve among other things, the ownership of a home or car, installment purchases, and salary and fringe benefit programs. One of the best ways to provide skill practice in this important component is to duplicate a simple sales contract obtained from a local company. Have each student read the copy of the contract and respond to a list of true/false statements relating to the material. The following might be sample statements.

1. You can pay the balance of the contract obligations at any time without penalty or interest. _____

2. The monthly payment is $38.50 to be paid on the first of each month at 1615 Lewis Street. _____

3. The interest on the unpaid balance will be figured at 12 percent. _____

O.

The ability to read and follow directions of a recipe for different types of foods is an important and desired skill. This practice can be obtained by duplicating a recipe and providing exercises which are of the completion type. By providing answer cards for each exercise the lesson can be self-corrective in nature. The following is a sample recipe along with a series of completion statements.

Alice's Spanish Hamburger

Ingredients:

1 pound lean hamburger	½ teaspoon salt
1 medium onion, diced	dash of pepper
5 cups cooked large elbow macaroni	dash of chili powder
1 8-oz. can tomato sauce	¼ teaspoon garlic salt

Cook hamburger, onion, salt, pepper, chili powder, and garlic salt in an electric skillet for about twenty minutes. Drain off liquid. Add the macaroni and tomato sauce and simmer on low heat for 10 minutes. Serve hot.

1. Use one _____ oz. can of tomato sauce.
2. The four seasonings used are _____,
   _____, _____, _____.
3. The total cooking time for the recipe is _____ minutes.
4. An _____ skillet is needed.
5. You should simmer the food on _____ heat.

P.

Floor plans of familiar buildings such as the school or library are interesting and provocative documents for most students. Some occupations in the building industry require proficiency in this skill. Students can gain meaningful practice in attaining understanding of floor plans by studying simple drawings and completing pertinent questions relating to the document. The school board architect or the school superintendent may have copies of selected floor plans which may be available for your use. Compose several completion statements which require the reader to state such information as length and width of rooms, outside dimensions of the building, and square feet of floor space.

Q.

All persons who drive an automobile have need to study and use the information derived from road maps of various types. There are many types of data which need to be processed by the reader such as distances between two cities, size of cities and counties, location of cities, familiar landmarks, and related data. One of the better strategies to improve the skill is to supply each student with a map of your state obtained from a service station or a book store. Ask the students to study the map closely and complete a matching exercise similar to the following. (Make two extra items for the second column to force the student to discriminate).

1. Distance from Anthony to Pratt	a. Independence
2. Name of the highest mountain in the state	b. Pierson City
	c. 25
3. Number of the major east-west turnpike in the state	d. I-20
	e. I-70
4. The city with the largest population	f. Ottawa
5. The city which is the county seat of Montgomery County	g. Oread

R.

Activities which help students to utilize information in grocery and discount store advertisements can be achieved through the careful analysis and study of various ads which appear daily in your local newspaper. Various investigative questions such as the following may be used to require the reader to study details and make comparisons between and among prices and services offered by different businesses. Samples of such questions may be as follows:

1. According to the ads, which grocery offers a pound of Swift's Premium bacon at the lowest price?

2. If you needed to purchase 10 lbs. of sugar, 1 loaf of rye bread, and ½ gallon of 2% milk, at which store would you shop for the lowest price?

3. At which stores could you purchase a Huffy bicycle?

S.

The careful study of the different types of road signs is an important aspect of safe highway driving. Signs have different shapes and colors to denote various messages. The ability to conceptualize this information is one of the most vital of the work related reading skills. In order to develop these skills, you may wish to ask permission from the state driver's license examiner to duplicate pictures of various road signs from the state driver's license manual. Below the signs on a piece of paper list several multiple-choice statements. The following may be illustrative.

1. Round signs generally mean (a) stop; (b) railroad tracks ahead; (c) slow; (d) yield.
2. Stop signs are painted which color? (a) red; (b) green; (c) yellow; (d) white.
3. A sign indicating that the driver should yield is what shape? (a) round; (b) square; (c) diamond-shaped; (d) triangle.

T.

Many adults of all ages and abilities encounter difficulties in the work related reading skill of following directions for assembling household and recreation articles such as pieces of furniture, bicycles, and exercise equipment. Many of these items come unassembled in boxes and require assembling by the purchaser. You could duplicate a set of directions for the set-up of a storage shelf. After your students have had a chance to read the information, ask them to respond to several true/false statements such as the following.

1. The bottom shelf should be glued first.
2. All shelves should be nailed and glued.
3. Rub-on varnish stain by Minwax should be used for the final touch.

Summary

Students who graduate from the 12th grade must be proficient in home and work related reading assignments if they are to pass competency examinations and be successful in pursuing various occupations. There are dozens of reading tasks in this important area such as those requiring the completion of various forms and applications, following directions on labels and cans, and shopping the ads in the daily paper.

There are diverse ways of evaluating a given student's ability in this area. A survey of some of these methods is included in this chapter. Those students who demonstrate limitation in these skills should be given practice for improvement through the use of one or more of the 20 suggestions listed at the close of the chapter.

REFERENCES

1. Alexander, J. Estill and others. *Teaching Reading.* Boston: Little, Brown and Company, 1979, Chapter 10.

2. Cushenbery, Donald C. *Reading Improvement Through Diagnosis, Remediation, and Individualized Instruction.* West Nyack: Parker Publishing Company, Inc., 1977. Chapter 9.

3. Mangrum, Charles T. and Forgan, Harry W. *Developing Competencies in Teaching Reading.* Columbus: Charles E. Merrill Publishing Company, 1979. Module 6.

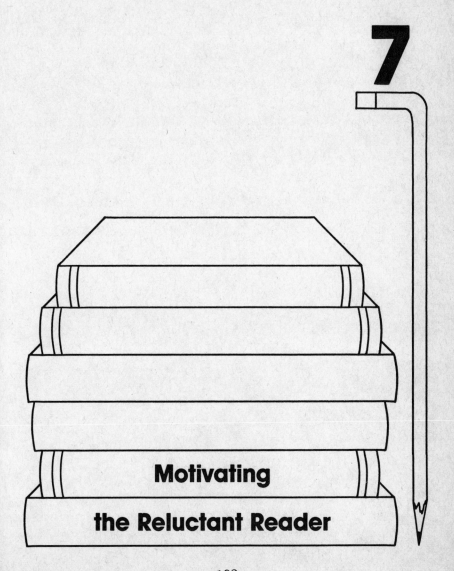

7

Motivating
the Reluctant Reader

One of the questions frequently asked by many educators and noneducators is "why do some students learn to read successfully while other students do not learn to read efficiently?" As indicated in an earlier chapter, there are a number of reasons why students don't learn to read at an acceptable level. Many people believe that one of the major reasons is a lack of motivation. The assignment of a given set of materials to be read by all students is not sufficient motivation for many learners to read. Many students do not read what has been assigned, regardless of the threat of tests or other consequences that might be enumerated by the instructor.

One often observes students in a classroom who are reading with enthusiasm and eagerness while students in another class appear to be reading only with minimal interest. Your responsibility as the teacher for building motivation is a very serious one. The topic of motivation has received very little attention in professional literature, even though the subject is crucial to all reading instruction.

In order to provide important information relating to this strategic topic, the following aspects of motivation are described and explained in this chapter: the importance and meaning of motivation; causes of lack of interest in reading; practical procedures for motivating problem readers; and ways to create a lifelong desire for reading with *your* students. A summary is provided at the close of the chapter along with a list of references for further reading.

IMPORTANCE AND MEANING OF MOTIVATION

Almost every task performed by a human being is motivated by some desire to improve, to challenge, or to impress other people. In the area of learning, the student must be motivated to gain new experiences that will enrich his/her life. One of the most important ways of securing new information and knowledge is through the printed word. Thus, if students are to gain new knowledge, they must be motivated to read widely.

The degree to which students read materials will be dependent upon the degree and kind of motivation provided by the teacher. If the *only* reason for reading is to secure information to pass a test, the level of desire will be at a lower stage than is satisfactory. Many studies of student behavior have pointed out that some older students may simply not read required reading assignments. One of the major reasons may be that they see no real reason for reading and don't really think the teacher will fail them. A few students will not even be motivated by the stark reality of the prospect of having to complete a competency test before a diploma is issued.

Observers of human learners often speculate why the students in Mr. X's class read with eagerness and anticipation, while the readers in Mr. Y's class dislike reading and fail to develop any interest in the reading act. To understand the situation, one needs to study the important factors related to motivation in reading. Students who have a very low level of motivation have usually developed this attitude because of one or more circumstances. If you are to motivate the uninterested and reluctant reader, look carefully at these factors and make a decision regarding which of them may be important reason(s) for a student's low level of reading interest.

The following principles appear to be crucial to every teacher in understanding the real importance and meaning of motivation. Each of these should be understood and studied with regard to every student who may have a motivational problem in your classroom.

1. Very few students really want to fail. Teachers can modify curriculums and establish reward systems that will allow all students to receive some kind of reward for success in the reading act.

2. There are many physical aspects in the environment of the learner that may promote or hinder motivation to read. With this in mind, a careful assessment of each student's physical health should be undertaken to determine if there are any physical reasons for the lack of desire to learn. The physical structure of the classroom should also be assessed and analyzed with respect to room temperature, noise level, and other factors.

3. With appropriate instruction, the level of student curiosity can be greatly heightened. Many students have a natural curiosity. This feature should always be maximized in the classroom setting. Accordingly, you should have much variety in your teaching and strive to meet each student's needs.

4. Much stress should be placed with older students on the area of meeting the needs of everyday reading assignments such as passing a driver's test, filling out an application blank, and reading the "Help Wanted" ads in the paper. These are everyday reading needs of adolescents and can provide an important incentive for students to read. In all cases, emphasize that the reading assignments you give are, in many ways, related to the kinds of reading skills your students will need when they leave school.

5. Lack of interest in reading could be an important cause of inefficient reading on the part of many middle and upper grade students. Because there is a significant relationship between interest in reading and reading ability, much attention should be given to ways of building reading interest levels of students. Somehow, reading must be developed as a

natural act on the part of those learners who are in a classroom.

**6. Teachers must understand that there are other
factors in a student's life that influence motivation for
reading.** Some recent studies appear to indicate that some
teenagers may spend as much as 30 hours a week watching
television. While some television programs help motivate a
student to read, others may not achieve this result. It would
behoove us, then, to work closely with television stations in
developing cooperative programs that will help the student to
build his reading interests.

**7. The aid of parents and all other adults should be
enlisted for interacting with our students in the process of
building and maintaining an interest in reading.** School
authorities might publish bulletins of various types containing
information on how parents might help their children develop
greater reading interests. These would include being a good
role model for the child, providing books, and establishing a
good learning and reading environment in the home. Some
learning specialists maintain that the levels of motivation for
reading of a young student may be influenced more by television and the home environment than we once thought.

**8. There are many ways of motivating students to in-
crease desire for reading.** Each student will be affected by a
different set of factors. Therefore, if we are to motivate students, it must be done on an individual basis. A careful assessment of the overall learning habits of the pupil must be
undertaken. The application of one or more of the techniques
described later in this chapter may be utilized in individual
cases.

**9. Teachers must understand that they may be one of
the most important role models in the lives of the students
who come to their classrooms.** Unfortunately, a few teachers give the impression that they are not interested in reading. If this is the case, the observant student feels that he/she
does not need to develop a motivation for reading widely.

In summary, motivation is a key factor in the remediation and correction of reading deficiencies. Unless a student feels the need to read and achieves some kind of success in the reading act, he/she will never develop the attitude that reading is important to be successful in life. The careful evaluation of each student's reading interests and attitudes is important if programs building motivation are to succeed. Each teacher must be a role model and use appropriate techniques in individual cases if students are to develop an attitude of heightened interest in pursuing assignments that call for reading.

CAUSES OF LACK OF INTEREST IN READING

There are many factors that might relate to a student's lack of motivation for reading. An older student who is a virtual nonreader and has little interest in reading probably has arrived at that stage because of several reasons, rather than for any one cause. There are, however, at least seven major factors relating to the level of interest that a given reader might exhibit. These are intelligence, socio-economic status, physiological factors, success and achievement, peer acceptance, student curiosity, and reading habits. Each of these is described in this section.

I. Intelligence appears to play a major part in determining what a student will read and the level of interest with which he/she will engage in the total act of reading and learning.

Numerous studies seem to indicate that there is an increasingly high correlation between the level of intelligence and the reading ability as the student grows older. There appears to be good evidence that students with higher I.Q.'s read books that are broader in nature and more difficult. The more gifted student tends to read in many different subject areas. The students with lower levels of intelligence tend to read only what is directly assigned to them and have fewer reading interests.

The less able student has more difficulty with the reading act and, therefore, avoids tasks that call for much oral and silent reading. A student who has very limited interests in reading should be evaluated with respect to his/her general level of intelligence. This action is not to suggest that there is no way of building a high level of interest with less intelligent students. However, it presents a challenge to the teacher to establish reward systems that will allow the less able student to be immediately successful in the reading environment.

II. **Though the results of research studies seem to be in conflict with regard to the relationship between a learner's socio-economic background and his/her level of reading interest, there does appear to be a slight positive correlation between socio-economic status and the number and kind of books that are read.**

If parents cannot afford to buy their children a large number of books and provide an appropriately stimulating atmosphere at home, they will naturally not develop the kind of desirable reading interests that might be developed in a home where many books and such stimulation is present. In many instances, children do not have a suitable physical environment in which to study, read books, and develop wide interests in reading. In assessing the levels of reading interest of your students, it would be well to gain some information relative to each individual learner's socio-economic background. You need to develop activities that will help the child compensate for an inadequate socio-economic atmosphere.

III. **There is a very significant relationship between the physiological status of learners and their level of learning interest.**

If students are to make effective progress in their reading and learning endeavors, they must be rested, well-nourished, and placed in a classroom setting that has adequate furniture, lighting and temperature. A very careful assessment of each learner's physical health should be undertaken by school authorities. Many other students are involved in illegal drugs and personal problems of various types that may prevent them from developing an interest in reading. Students who have severe problems of these types may need to be recommended for counseling by school and public agencies. Only after physical and emotional conditions have been improved can one expect any increase in the level of motivation to read.

IV. If students are to build desirable levels of reading interests, they must be placed in learning environments where success and achievement are possible.

In far too many instances, teachers give the same assignments to all of the students in a given class. Some of the students have not been able to read the textbook and answer the questions that the teacher has prepared. For example, the student's instructional reading level might have been only at the seventh grade level, while the reading level of the textbook was at the tenth grade level. If this is the case, the student obviously will find the reading act to be unpleasant and certainly will not strive to build further interest in reading and learning. Teachers need to remember the time-honored expression that "Nothing breeds success like success."

If this feeling is to be evidenced by the students in your classroom, individualized assignments will need to be constructed for students who have varying reading abilities. Most students will develop favorable levels of interest if they are given assignments that they can read and understand.

V. In today's society, proficiency in reading skills is generally considered a requirement for success in any occupation.

Most parents, relatives, and employers expect and demand literacy. Nearly all students want to succeed. The fear of failure and of not meeting the requirements of society is a powerful motivator for many pupils. Some sociologists such as Dr. Robert Havighurst contend that reading qualifies as a developmental task. According to Havighurst,* "a developmental task arises at or about a certain period of life of the individual, successful achievement of which leads to his/her hapiness and/or success of later tasks; while failure leads to unhappiness of the individual, disapproval by the society, and difficulty with later tasks." Very few students want disapproval.

VI. Student curiosity has much to do with the eventual level of reading interest of a given student.

While most learners have a natural curiosity about the world and would like to learn many different things about the environment, a few students apparently lack this particular characteristic. This deficiency may have been caused by a lack of stimulation in the home or by a general deprivation in the socio-economic environment. One can assess a student's level of curiosity with regard to reading and learning by visiting with the student or by administering a pencil and paper inventory of reading interests. By recording information about books and articles read, one will be able to get some idea of the child's level of curosity with respect to reading interests and attitudes. Probably the best informal technique is a well-structured conversation with the student to discover as much information as possible about his/her attitudes toward reading in general.

VII. Many students appear to be reluctant readers because they have never established positive reading habits.

They have never made reading a part of their everyday routine; thus, their level of interest is certainly below that

---

*Robert J. Havighurst, *Human Development and Education* (New York: Longmans, Green and Company, 1953), p. 2.

which is common to better and more able readers. The assessment of the general reading habits of the student can be made through the use of informal techniques such as incomplete sentences and reading interest inventories.

In summary, there are many factors that influence a given learner's desire to read. No one factor described in this section can be considered more important than any of the others. No doubt, several of these factors are responsible for a general low level of motivation for reading. It is important that you understand these factors and their relationship to the total reading act. Very few students really want to fail. For the student who has a very low level of motivation or interest in reading, the wise teacher attempts to isolate those factors that create the lack of motivation and attempts to enhance interest by using one or more of the procedures and methods described in the next section.

PRACTICAL PROCEDURES FOR MOTIVATING PROBLEM READERS

There are dozens of classroom tested activities that every teacher can use to spur motivation in reading. The purpose of this section is to amplify some of these suggestions in order for *you* to use them in your classroom *today*. The suggestions have been grouped into three major areas. They are general reading interests, motivating students in the language arts, and using the library to enhance motivation.

I. Building General Reading Interests

A. In order to enlarge the reading interests of your students, compile and distribute individual interest inventories to each of your students for completion. The answers to the questions on this inventory will give you some insight into the students' present interests or lack of interest. If, for any reason, you suspect that many of your students cannot read the printed inventory, you may wish to ask each student the questions in an oral manner—perhaps in an individual interview that you might conduct. The following is a series of questions that might be included in an interest inventory.

1. Besides your daily assignment, what other kinds of materials do you read?
2. Do you read the daily newspaper?
3. What magazines do you like best?
4. What do you like about them?
5. Who are your favorite heroes from either the present or the past?
6. Name three of your favorite television programs.
7. Do you listen to the radio? What programs do you like?
8. How many hours per week do you watch television?
9. If you could spend a day in the library, what would probably be the first kind of book you would like to read?
10. If you wanted to write a book, what would be its title?

After studying the information collected from the inventories, one could base further instruction on the data collected. For example, you may wish to find high interest-low vocabulary books in the areas of interest that a given student has indicated.

B. You, the teacher, must serve as a role model for the student in generating interest for books. The attitude of the teacher can make a tremendous difference in the student's interest in reading and learning. Students soon sense when a teacher has little or no enthusiasm for books. The attitude of the teacher, for example, will dictate how much interest students will have in poetry, in science experiments, in making a cabinet, or playing a game in physical education class. Make frequent reference to the books and other materials you are reading.

C. The classroom atmosphere will be a leading factor in whether or not students are motivated and interested in reading. A dull, drab room with long lines of brown desks, no bulletin boards, and only a few books is hardly an environment to stimulate interest in reading. Conversely, rooms where the furniture is arranged in a comfortable fashion, with interesting bulletin boards, and many books attractively displayed will serve to heighten interest in reading. The dust covers from new books that have arrived in the library and pertain to a given content area can be arranged on the bulletin board in the room or rooms where a particular subject is taught.

D. You can also heighten the motivation of students by reading *aloud* to them. Young children in elementary school like to have teachers read to them and despite myths to the contrary, older students, even high school students, enjoy a teacher who has a good speaking voice and who is willing to share new and interesting books in the field they are teaching. You, for example, may want to read a part of a book and stop with the comment that perhaps the students might enjoy reading the rest on their own. Content teachers may wish to form reading clubs where interested students can share experiences they have encountered by reading books from a number of different sources. This could be a formal club that would meet on a regular basis or it could be a club that would meet for a brief time during the regularly scheduled class. Schools that have activity periods might be able to accommodate this type of club easily.

E. One of the major ways of fostering interest in reading is that of ownership of books. Since paperback books are relatively inexpensive and are widely distributed, these kinds of materials might be the main source of reading matter for book distribution projects. You may wish to have a book exchange rack in your room. All students who would like to participate would bring one or more paperback books and place them on the rack. Each student may remove a paperback book from the rack if he/she brings one to replace the one that has been taken.

Students unable to afford books might participate in the *Reading Is Fundamental* program, which is taking place in many cities across America. Local civic groups typically sponsor the RIF projects. Information concerning the Reading Is Fundamental program can be secured by writing Reading Is Fundamental, c/o the Smithsonian Institute in Washington, D.C.

F. Curiosity in learning can be generated by such activities as special reading contests. Middle and upper grade teachers in some locations have used what is called the "book worm" idea. Under this plan, segments of a large simulated worm are cut from brown paper and the name of the book and reader are placed on each of the sections. When all of the sections are connected, an ever-lengthening bookworm is seen on the wall of the classroom. If students become particularly eager to read books the bookworm might well extend out into the hall and all the way to the principal's office. This not only stimulates interest in the room of the teacher who originated the idea, but in the entire building as well.

G. The use of guest speakers can have a positive effect on building reading interests. Guest speakers might be authors of books that are in the library, or if not authors, they may be scientists, local business executives, or officials who perform experiments, show films, or advertise other kinds of printed material. Some companies publish different bulletins and booklets on various phases of their history. Many learners like to read this type of material. If students see these industries as a future source of employment, they may be inspired to read these and related materials on a particular industry.

H. The establishment of a sustained silent reading period as a part of your instructional reading program may be a way of generating interest. If your class meets from 1:00 to 1:50 p.m. each day, you may wish to schedule the period from 1:00 to 1:15 on Fridays as your sustained silent reading period. If the sustained silent reading period is to be successful, you must have many books available. Regulations concerning this period should be outlined and understood by all students. All students may select a piece of reading material and have it ready at the beginning of the period. Obviously, they are not to disturb or bother other people since the activity will be a strictly individualized concern.

I. Reading interests can be heightened considerably through the use of leisure reading files. These files can be constructed by each content teacher. The material and theme of the files would parallel the content subject being taught.

The file consists of a cardboard box approximately 12 inches deep, 20 inches long, and 14 inches wide. Cover the box with colorful paper or adhesive decorative material. Devise file dividers from pieces of stiff cardboard and place information tabs on the tops of the file. In the different areas of the file box, place articles, stories, poems, and other related materials that correlate with the topic typed on the top of the file folder. The daily newspaper might be the source for current event articles in the case of a social studies class. The literature teacher may wish to have a division that contains book reviews. The physical education teacher may want to have stories from newspapers relating to various sports events. At least one portion of the leisure reading file may be given over to creative original stories written by readers during the past or the current semester. Students will use the leisure reading file if they are trained to do so and if there is some kind of reward system connected with the activity. Extra credit

might be given to those students who make use of the classroom lesiure reading file.

II. Motivating Students in Language Arts

A. Meaningful creative writing activities can enhance
reading interests on the part of many students. You may wish
to give the last sentence of a creative story and ask them to
write the story or selection that precedes the final sentence.
For example, you may supply this sentence: "And that's why
we won third in the State Basketball Tournament." Or you
may wish to use a sentence like "That is why my bathtub was
filled with green Jello." Each student could create the story in
his/her own way.

B. Duplicate several copies of a familiar story, song, or
passage and leave out selected descriptive words. Invite students to supply words of their own for the original words. Ask
volunteers to read their newly created selections for the class.

C. After studying the various propaganda techniques
(such as card stacking, identification with prestige, bandwagon, plain folks, etc.), supply your class with copies of the
daily newspaper. Ask them to find one or two examples of
each of these propaganda techniques. An alternative to this
activity would be placing an object such as the overhead
projector on the teacher's desk and asking students to create
advertising copy for the item by purposely using as many
propaganda techniques as they can recall.

D. Content area teachers may wish to have their students look at video tapes or films of various subjects dealing
with the content area under consideration. Ask students to
write a review of the presentation stating what they thought
was good about the presentation and what they thought could
have been improved. If they think the presentation could
have been improved, they should be asked to describe how
they would have changed the script had they been the pro-
ducer and/or director.

E. One of the best ways of motivating students to read is to have them read the parts of a play or story. They should emphasize in their oral reading how they think a particular character or personality said the words. These plays and stories could be recorded for playback to the entire class if the actors and actresses give their permission. Depending on the age of the learners involved, puppets or marionettes might be useful.

F. Many students become interested in textbook and classwide reading materials by actually corresponding with the author or authors of the materials. Most authors are delighted to hear from readers who are using the books they have written and will correspond with the students. Perhaps the students would like to submit a list of questions to them about the book or about their personal interests as a writer. They may wish to send a tape along with their letter for the author or authors to respond to the class in person by this medium.

III. Using the School Library to Enhance Motivation

The school library is the hub of all learning in any particular setting. There are many opportunities for using the school library to stimulate reading and motivate students to engage in wide reading. The responsibility for utilizing the library does not lie solely with the media specialist or the librarian. Rather, it is the joint responsibility of all the teachers who use printed materials. The following are some school-tested activities for using the library to motivate students to read.

A. Individual teachers can establish miniature reading libraries within their own classrooms. A small library shelf can be set up to hold a number of books linked to the content area you are teaching. The books might be on loan from students, the school library, or the public library. A student in the class could be designated as the room librarian and be in charge of checking the books in and out of the room. Establish a book review file in which students who have read books would write three or four sentences on how they evaluated a given book. These could be placed in a file under the book and author's name. When students anticipated checking out particular books, they could look at the review cards to see what someone else had said about the book. This might prove to be a very valuable force in motivating reading, since the feelings of peers toward books or articles are terribly important to students. A small amount of time in each school week should be given to checking in and checking out books, as well as to short book reviews that individual students might make for the class.

B. Some students find printed materials boring. Today there are many companies that produce tapes that give a short review of books. The reviews lead up to a certain place in the story and the person recording the tape invites the listener to read the remainder of the story. Appendix A contains many of the media materials you might use for this and related purposes for motivating students to read. This, of course, would mandate that the school library become a true media center where tapes, videotapes, and recordings of various sorts are housed for use by students who are interested in further reading.

C. The media specialist using student aids could compile a notebook containing various cartoons clipped from the daily newspaper. The student could be encouraged to look at the cartoon and supply a caption for it. On the back of the original cartoon would be the caption that appeared in the newspaper. Students could compare their captions with the ones selected by the person who created the cartoon. All of the cartoons could be laminated and placed in the notebook. If students used the notebook and recorded any kind of responses, they could use a grease pencil. After they had completed the activity, they could erase the markings and many other students could use the same notebook.

D. Book reports and book reviews by students can be of great help in stimulating interest in books by other students. Unfortunately, book reports have a bad reputation in many professional circles because they have been used inappropriately by some teachers. Obviously, if a set number of long book reports is required each and every grading period, this practice will turn off many students and they certainly will not be motivated to read widely. Innovative and interested teachers can, however, use many variations of book reports to motivate reading. Here are a few classroom tested activities that have been used in various schools.

1. Compose a letter to a friend rcommending a certain book to him/her.

2. Conduct a panel discussion involving several students who have read the same book. Urge the participants to point out what they liked or disliked about the book. They perhaps could be encouraged to talk about how they would have written the book had they been the authors.

3. Give a sales talk acting as a sales person who is trying to sell the book to the class. Vivid dramatics can be used to urge students to buy and read this book immediately.

4. Select one of the characters from the book and act the part of the person in a brief presentation for the class. Those students who are particularly innovative might like to put on costumes for this presentation.

5. Some students who have art interests may wish to make a mural or a poster relating to a major episode in a book that is available in the room or school library.

6. Some students may prefer to read brief excerpts from a book available in the school library. Another alternative would be to duplicate brief excerpts and place them on cards in a review box in the library so that

students who look at the cards might become interested in reading the book in question.

7. Depending on the student group, a reader might prefer to act as a reporter from the local newspaper describing a particularly dramatic scene from the book.

8. Two students might wish to act as a reporter and a major character in a particular story. The reporter could ask the character various questions about his/her role in the story or play.

E. Media specialists within a school can cooperate with local television stations in obtaining scripts of upcoming television shows that dramatize books to be found in the school library. These scripts can be delivered by the specialist to various content teachers when the play or the television production centers around a book or subject that correlates with the content areas being taught by a given teacher. Some empirical research studies seem to indicate that the use of television to stimulate reading in books may have a more pronounced impact than was once thought.

F. The use of bibliotherapy by media specialists and content teachers may be an important aspect of motivating students to read. Though the value of bibliotherapy is under some debate among reading and learning specialists, it, nevertheless, provides positive results if used correctly. In its simplest terms, bibliotherapy promotes the placing of a book that has a theme designed to meet the immediate personal needs of the reader in the hands of this reader. An important publication called the *Bookfinder*, published by American Guidance Services, Inc. (Circle Pines, Minnesota 55014) is a very valuable source for finding books that relate to particular needs of students.

G. Many schools have public address systems for making announcements to students at various times during the day. One of the most fascinating ways of generating interest in reading is by setting aside a short time during the announcement period on a particular day for "advertising" new books that have arrived in the library. Perhaps only three or four sentences need to be said about the book. As many as ten to fifteen books can be advertised each Friday. If these announcements are given by the students themselves, it will have a greater impact on building motivation for reading than if a school authority gives the announcements.

H. The librarian and/or media specialist can cooperate with the editor of the school newspaper in providing a short list of descriptions of books recently cataloged in the library. Perhaps various students in the school could take turns providing brief reviews of the books. Excerpts from letters or tapes that have been received from authors of books might also be included in newspaper articles.

I. The school media specialist might conduct a survey of student requests for magazines and books. The one-page questionnaire or survey could be given to all students, for example, in the English class. The survey sheet would indicate the titles of the magazines now available in the library. A place would be provided for students to list other magazines that might be considered for subscriptions by the media specialist and authorities. This type of information may be helpful in ordering magazines for the next school year.

J. Library staffs should always have a lighted, glassed-in display area for introducing new books to students. In the display case would be the dust covers and other advertising relative to new and exciting books which have arrived at the library. These should be changed frequently so students will get as wide an exposure as possible to these books. Many times student committees are quite eager to undertake this kind of creative endeavor. They should be used in every case where it seems plausible and profitable.

K One of the most exciting methods for motivating students to read is the sponsorship of a reading club by the school library or media center. Depending on the ages of the students involved, readers might receive certificates with a red seal for reading 10 books, a blue seal for reading 15 books, and a gold seal for reading 20 books during a school year. Perhaps the certificates could be signed by the superintendent of schools or the director of the Board of Education to lend importance to the project. There are numerous ways of checking the validity of claims for books read. The use of one-page mini reports on the book might be used. Another method would be compiling brief summaries on each of the chapters of the book read. Book conferences might be employed if the media specialist and/or the content teachers would have student teachers or teacher aids available to help them with such a project.

L. Some schools motivate students to read by having a yearly contest to see which books are voted the most outstanding volumes of the year. The most popular, second most popular, and the third most popular books are chosen by a vote of the student body on pencil and paper ballot. If appropriate and convenient, the awards for these three books could be given to representatives of the publishers during the award assembly at the close of the school year. If the author or the authors of the books chosen could be present, this, of course, would be ideal and most interesting.

CREATING A LIFELONG DESIRE FOR READING IN YOUR STUDENTS

As indicated in this chapter, there are widely varying levels of reading interest on the part of students who attend a given school. There are numerous factors involved in determining motivation, and many students have various personal problems that may inhibit interest in reading. The importance of building motivation for the reading act should not be underestimated. It is the job of the *total* school faculty and not the responsibility of only one or two teachers.

The teacher as role model is a very important aspect of the whole process of motivation. Students, ideally, should meet a series of teachers during any given school day, all of whom exhibit a high level of desire to read and consider reading to be a very enjoyable and profitable activity. As indicated in the previous section, there are dozens of ways for building motivation in reading. The methods and procedures utilized by social studies teachers for motivating students to read, will in some ways, be different from those that may be profitably employed by the English teacher or the media specialist. The procedures used by any given teacher will depend on the teacher's personality and, indeed, the number and types of students being instructed. The general ability levels of the students along with their socio-economic backgrounds will be significant factors in determining what kinds of motivational procedures to use and for what length of time.

Despite the best intentions of the most intense, conscientious teacher, it is too idealistic to think that every student will develop a high level of motivation for reading. We as teachers, however, have a grave responsibility to our students to use as many profitable procedures and principles as possible to reach as many students as we can. Building a lasting love for reading and motivating students to read widely can be accomplished by using several of the procedures and techniques described earlier. In addition to these, all teachers should subscribe to the five principles explained in the following section.

1. Be sure you know the strengths and limitations of each student with respect to reading skills. Determine his/her present general level of interest in reading. Avoid placing them in reading environments that they find threatening. Assigning books that are too difficult or mandating long prescribed book reports will surely kill reading interest.

2. It is important to establish an easy, relaxed, and positive atmosphere for reading activities. Let your students know that you value reading and you hope they will share books with you as opportunities present themselves. The inclusion of a mini-library within your own classroom will do much to provide that kind of atmosphere.

3. Provide a special time period in the day's schedule when reading can be pursued. As indicated earlier, you may want to conduct an uninterrupted, sustained silent reading period during a given day of each school week. Students should always be given a purpose for reading and should understand why they should read a book and what information should be derived from the reading. By observing the students reading silently, you will be able to make any determinations about their skills in reading and to gain some kinds of information about their general level of motivation for the reading act.

4. Place a large number of reading materials in your classroom written on many different grade and interest levels. There are many publishers today who are publishing high interest-low vocabulary books in almost every content area. Numerous publishers, for example, are publishing content area books with 10th or 11th grade reading interests, but 5th or 6th grade reading levels. You would do well to promote the idea that all books in your classroom have roughly equal importance and that reading one book is no less or no more important than reading another book. Students will be motivated to read if they can find materials with which they will have some success. Conversely, they will not read with any degree of interest if they are forced to read from a limited number of very difficult books.

5. A number of different avenues should be pursued that would allow a student to demonstrate his/her likes and/or dislikes about books and stories. Brief written reports, newspaper stories, bulletin board displays, or oral book reports might be used for this purpose. Unfortunately, a few teachers convey the idea that there is only one interpretation that can be given to a story and when students discover this condition to be true, their interests in reading are seriously diminished. A positive, relaxed atmosphere allowing students to make

their own comments about books will certainly cultivate a desire on the part of many students to read widely and enjoy reading.

Summary

Motivation is a very important aspect of the total reading environment present in every school. There are many reasons why some students have a high level of reading interest while others seemingly don't possess this interest. There are numerous factors that are important in the assessment of motivation of reading. Some of these are level of intelligence, socio-economic background, physiological factors, success and achievement, peer acceptance, student curiosity, and level of reading habits. Each student who displays a below-average level of reading motivation should be evaluated with respect to his/her strengths and limitations in these various areas. One or more of the classroom tested techniques discussed in this chapter can be highly useful to you with many students in improving reading motivation. Creating a lifelong desire for reading is the responsibility of all teachers and not any one teacher. The five principles discussed at the close of the chapter should be understood and inculcated in the teaching program of every teacher using printed materials in the classroom.

REFERENCES

1. Bush, Clifford, L. and Heubner, Mildred H. *Strategies for Reading in The Elementary School.* New York: Macmillan Publishing Co., Inc., 1979. Ch. 8.

2. Cushenbery, Donald C. *Reading Improvement Through Diagnosis, Remediation and Individualized Instruction.* West Nyack: Parker Publishing Company, Inc., 1977. Ch. 2.

3. Havighurst, Robert J. *Human Development and Education*. New York: Longmans, Green and Company, 1953.

4. Hill, Walter R. *Secondary School Reading Process, Program, Procedure*. Boston: Allyn and Bacon, Inc., 1979. Ch. 2.

8

Meeting

the Individual Needs

of All Pupils for

Enlarging Reading

Competencies

One of the most perplexing instructional problems for any teacher is assessing the learning needs of each student and providing appropriate and practical strategies for reading skill development. Teachers need to understand what skills are needed and desired, the precise diagnostic instruments to employ, and how to provide the right prescriptive lesson to meet the individual needs of learners. This instructional responsibility is particularly formidable when one encounters a large number of students in a group situation.

The purposes of this chapter are to provide classroom tested suggestions with regard to the following topics: (1) using diagnostic procedures to assess each child's skill levels; (2) finding the right method for each learner; and (3) practical means of meeting individual needs in a group situation.

USING DIAGNOSTIC PROCEDURES
TO ASSESS EACH CHILD'S SKILL LEVELS

The diagnostic component of a reading instructional curriculum is vital for a number of reasons. After having constructed the body of skills and competencies desired with respect to a group of learners, one must establish a program of evaluation to assess the degree to which the program objectives have been met. The resulting data will provide meaningful information relating to those parts of the teaching strategies that should be maintained or altered. In some cases, materials may need to be changed or different approaches used that emphasize several learning modalities.

Diagnostic procedures also enable a teacher to determine the individual reading strengths and limitations of various pupils. These data will help in the process of making decisions relative to the identification of those students needing further diagnosis and subsequent remedial teaching. The final determination with regard to matters of this type should be made only after careful analysis of test results from several sources has been completed.

Besides the purposes described in the previous section, there are other reasons for undertaking an extensive program of reading diagnosis with your students. Each is explained in the following section.

A. Results of diagnostic testing can be utilized in understanding significant research in your classroom as well as the total school setting. These data may help to answer such questions as: (1) To what degree are our students competent in the various phonic analysis skills? and (2) What comprehension skill strands need further reinforcement in the total school reading program?

B. Analysis of reading abilities may be quite helpful in determining the types of hardware and software materials that should be used in the teaching-learning environment. (Unfortunately, in too many instances, materials and programs are purchased *before* the results of evaluation instruments are studied.)

C. Evaluative test data can also be utilized to help teachers group students for remedial instruction. As much as possible, readers should be taught in individual situations. There are occasions when it is justifiable to place several students together for teaching if they have *similar* deficiencies. A careful study of the profile sheets (which have been described in previous chapters) will provide significant insight with regard to the exact names of pupils who need further help in important reading skill areas.

If one is to use diagnostic data to meet the instructional needs of individual students, several principles need to be kept in mind.

1. *Diagnostic procedures should be undertaken on a continuous as well as a periodic basis.* Since careful visual observation can yield important information, the daily work with each learner adds much valuable data to the evaluation process.
2. *The analysis of an individual learner's reading skill competencies should utilize both formal and informal techniques and instruments.* As noted in Appendix B, there are many outstanding commercial diagnostic reading tests. These should be used along with several of the classroom tested teacher constructed tests described in Chapter 1.
3. *The status of a student's reading skill development level should be determined only after a pattern of scores has been studied.* Different strategies emphasize various facets of the reading process, thus an overall assessment must consider data from a number of sources.
4. *One of the goals of the evaluation program should be the development of self-appraisal on the part of all students.* Individual improvement will not be realized until the student has a clear understanding and *personal commitment* to improve. For example, Henry will be much more aware of word attack deficiencies by hearing word miscues on a tape as opposed to having them pointed out on paper by the test examiner.

As discussed earlier, diagnostic procedures form one of the most important aspects of any reading instruction program. The principles and practices described in the previous section should be helpful to you in the planning, development, and implementation of reading analysis procedures.

FINDING THE RIGHT METHOD FOR EACH LEARNER

The next important step following reading diagnosis is finding the right method to employ with a student who has demonstrated reading deficiencies. If one uses the medical model of *diagnosis, prescription, and continuing supervision,* the aspect of prescriptive lessons may be the *most important* segment of the total instructional program. Since there are literally *dozens* of diagnostic procedures and *hundreds* of instructional devices and strategies available to the reading teacher, the selection of the *right* method for a disabled reader is no small undertaking. Obviously, the degree of correction and integration that exists between analysis and correction should be a relevant concern for any reading educator. The rate of remediation realized by the student will be greatly affected by the "rightness" of the choice of teaching strategies applied. While the final determination of teaching strategies is a subjective matter, there are several considerations that should be implemented in making these important judgments. Think about the following aspects as you engage in this important activity.

1. *There is no one method or material that is equally successful with all problem readers.* The reading skill patterns of students are sufficiently different; thus, what one learner needs is not what another should have prescribed. Claims of authors and publishers relating to the universality of their materials should be studied most carefully.

2. *A variety of methods should be employed for a brief period of time with attention given to such aspects as students' attitude, demonstrated skill improvement, and ease of use of the procedure.* Due to the fact that readers have preferred learning modalities and react differently to many and varied teaching approaches, the use of a multi-faceted set of strategies is urgent and necessary.

3. *A carefully designed evaluative process should be structured and implemented to monitor the strengths and limitations of a given instructional approach.* After having determined appropriate objectives and competencies, one must be sure that the total program is producing desired results. As explained in earlier chapters, such analysis should be broad in scope and encompass such aspects as

observation, commercial tests, interviews, and teacher-made instruments.

4. *The "right" method for a given learner should allow for maximum growth and success and for further development of the ego.* The procedure chosen should be one that would provide for the charting of reading progress. The assignment segments should be of sufficient size and magnitude to allow the student to move along at his/her own rate. Progress plotters consisting of grid sheets may be useful for showing reading growth.

PRACTICAL MEANS OF MEETING INDIVIDUAL NEEDS IN A GROUP SITUATION

One of the most significant instructional problems encountered by most teachers is that of meeting the individual instructional needs of a learner who is part of a large group class setting. The amount of time available for meeting the individual needs may be very limited if the class is large. *If you are a content teacher who instructs five to six large classes a day, the job of helping individual learners with reading difficulties is challenging.*

There are some techniques and strategies that you can employ to help problem readers in large classes. The following suggestions have been utilized by successful teachers for many years.

1. *List the names of the students in each class who are in serious need of reading remediation.* Very early in the school year or semester you could administer a commercial or teacher-made test to determine how well each student functions in several important skill areas such as word analysis, vocabulary, comprehension, and study skills. This information may be readily available from the data derived from a reading achievement test that has been recently administered in your school. In the absence of these data, you may wish to administer an informal instrument such as a cloze test or a group comprehension

test constructed from sections found in the class textbook. A critical score should be established for each and every one of the tests. Students who make scores below the critical levels would be identified for further help (e.g., those who get less than 38 on a 50 blank cloze test and/or those who achieve less than 74 percent on a comprehension test). (The cloze and other tests are explained in earlier chapters of this volume).

2. *Place students who have common reading deficiencies in small instructional groups for intensive practice on one particular skill strand.* While the majority of the class members complete a given written assignment, you could, for example, provide lesson sheets for three or four students who need intensive help in interpretative comprehension skills. The next day, you could work with another small group that needs further help in structural analysis. By rotating the groups, it is possible to render much aid to troubled youth in an individual or small group setting on a regular basis.

3. *The use of multilevel assignments may be useful in meeting the individual reading instructional needs of students.* In utilizing a common set of materials for a given class, invariably students will not be proficient in all of the four levels of comprehension. Typically, the better readers will understand all of the levels while less able readers will have problems with the critical and creative levels. Accordingly, it would be advisable to assign more of the written critical and creative questions to the better readers and designate the literal and interpretative questions for the less able readers. If better readers wish to answer the questions for *all* four levels, they should be allowed to do so.

4. *One may wish to use varied level textbooks for use with those students who have grave reading deficiencies.* Some publishers (such as Globe and Follett) are now publishing textbooks for the content areas that contain grade level concepts (such as 11th or 12th grade) but are written at the

6th and 7th grade readability levels. These books can be quite useful and practical for the reluctant reader.

5. *The construction and use of study guides for the less able reader is an excellent tool for meeting individual learning needs.* Many successful teachers make use of study guides for helping students pronounce words, find key words and phrases, and derive significant meanings. The guide might contain the following features: (a) significant words and phrases and their meanings; (b) an overview of the total chapter or unit; and (c) brief summaries of each section that are written at a readability level much lower than grade level.

These guides are of significant help to problem readers since they are written at a level they can understand and pinpoint the precise information they should remember. While such aids should be handed to the less able readers, the better readers will also find them helpful. To facilitate construction of such guides, several teachers who instruct a common content subject may wish to divide the writing assignment among the various participants. The guides should be revised periodically according to suggestions and constructive criticism received from the students and teachers who use the materials.

Summary

There are various purposes for reading diagnostic processes. The data derived from the various procedures should be used to select materials, group students, and undertake research studies. Several principles need to be kept in mind in utilizing diagnostic test data. There is a "right" method for each student; however, you should remember that several aspects should be studied before making decisions regarding method selection. Providing for individual needs in a group situation is a challenging assignment for any teacher. The five suggestions described at the close of the chapter should be of much help to you in this regard.

REFERENCES

1. Bader, Lois. A. *Reading Diagnosis and Remediation in Classroom and Clinic*. New York: Macmillan Publishing Co., Inc., 1980. Ch. 5.

2. Burns, Paul C. and Roe, Betty D. *Informal Reading Assessment*. Chicago: Rand McNally Publishing Company, 1980. Section 2.

3. Otto, Wayne and others. *Focused Reading Instruction*. Reading, Massachusetts: Addison-Wesley Publishing Company, 1974. Ch. 11.

APPENDIX A

Selected Materials for Corrective Reading

1. *Adult Readers*

   Reader's Digest Services, Inc.
   Educational Division
   Pleasantville, New York 10570

   Vocabulary Development
   Word Attack Skills
   Comprehension Skills

   Junior High-Adult

   Twelve readers offer mature-interest, low vocabulary stories of courage, daring self-reliance and adventure. There are short, practical exercises after each story in easy-to-read type and with colorful illustrations to reinforce basic reading skills.

2. *Advanced Skills in Reading*

   The MacMillan Co.
   60 Fifth Avenue
   New York, New York 10011

   Book 1—Grade 7
   Book 2—Grade 8

   Aims at improving reading through step-by-step skill development and practice.

3. *Career Awareness Program*

   King Features
   Department 1344
   235 East 45 Street
   New York, New York 10017

   Grades 5-9

   Comic books, games, posters and exercises present serious, factually detailed information about fifteen career clusters as described by the United States Office of Education. The training and education requirements for each are explained as well as the advantages and disadvantages of each cluster. Opportunity for advancement and fulfillment are illustrated.

4. *Gates-Peardon Reading*   Teacher's College Press
   Exercises   Teacher's College, Columbia Univ.
                          525 W. 120 Street
                          New York, New York 10027

Introductory: Level A&B—Grade 2
Preparatory: Level A&B—Grade 3
Elementary: Level A&B—Grade 4
Intermediate: Level A&B—Grade 5
Advanced: Level A&B—Grade 6

This series is designed to strengthen students' ability to pick out main ideas, note and recall details, and understand directions.

5. *Graphs and Surveys*   Xerox Education Publications
                          Education Center
                          Columbus, Ohio 43216

Study Skills

Junior High-Adult

This program is an introduction to interpreting and preparing graphs and surveys, assembling information, evaluating, organizing, and then translating it into graphic form.

6. *Grow in Word Power*   Reader's Digest Services, Inc.
                          Education Division
                          Pleasantville, New York 10570

Vocabulary Development

Junior High-Adult

Fun exercises that help students acquire a larger vocabulary and improve spelling skills. The word games include: Match words with meanings, juggling letters, double spellings, get the meaning from context, chess-type game with words, word analogies, and geographical analogies.

7. *Help Yourself to Improve*   Reader's Digest Services, Inc.
   Your Reading   Educational Division
                          Pleasantville, New York 10570

Comprehension Skills

Junior High-Adult

"Want-to-read" selections in a do-it-yourself format emphasizing speeded comprehension. Each selection contains an essay, a narrative, a biographical sketch and a factual report. Each reader features a word count for every selection, professional tips on previewing, adjusting reading speed and increasing comprehension. A comprehension quiz follows each selection.

8. *King Classics Libraries*   King Features
                                       Department 1344
                                       235 East 45 Street
                                     New York, New York 10017

Grades 5-12

Designed to awaken the "bookworm" inside so many reluctant readers. Developed to take fear and tension out of the "reading chore." Three full King Classics Libraries; read-along cassettes; sequentially designed skill-building work books for each library; and new sound/filmstrip classics.

Library 1	*Library 2*	*Library 3*
Robinson Crusoe	*A Christmas Carol*	*Alice in Wonderland*
Moby Dick	*The Adventures of*	*The Black Arrow*
20,000 Leagues	*Huck Finn*	*Five Weeks in a*
Under the Sea	*Around the World*	*Balloon*
& more	*in 80 Days*	*Great Expectations*
	Ivanhoe	& more
	& more	

9. *Listen and Read*   Educational Development
                               Laboratories, Inc.
                               1221 Avenue of The Americas
                               New York, New York 10020

Comprehension Skills
Study Skills
Listening Skills

Junior High-Adult

This program consists of set D for a fourth grade reading

level; set GHI for levels 7, 8, 9; set JKL for levels 10, 11, 12; set
MN for Adult and college. There are thirty lessons with scripts
for accompanying recordings, workbooks, and lesson books.
Each lesson begins with an introductory sketch, dialogue, or
sequence of sound effects to capture interest and attention. The
narrator introduces the students to the skill or concept being
dealt with and then guides them through listening and workbook exercises in which they gain practice in various phases of
the skill or concept.

10. *Picto-Cabulary Series*   Barnell-Loft Ltd.
                                       958 Church Street
                                       Baldwin, New York 11510

Vocabulary Development

Intermediate-Senior High

Two sets are used to stimulate pupils' interest in words and
to enlarge their own vocabularies. Each set is of equal difficulty.
Each set is made up of two copies of each of six different titles
for a total of twelve booklets. Worksheets and a teacher's manual are included with each set.

11. *Audio Reading Progress*   Educational Progress Corporation
    Laboratory   Division of Educational
                                       Development Corporation
                                       P. O. Box 45663
                                       Tulsa, Oklahoma 74145

Skill Sheets and cassettes. Basic skills, self-directed, immediate feedback.

12. *Comprehension Audio*   Reader's Digest Services, Inc.
    Lessons   Educational Division
                                       Pleasantville, New York 10570

Oral Reading Skills
Comprehension Skills

Primary-Adult

A specific reading skill is developed in each audio lesson, such
as recognizing main ideas or noting sequence of events. This

program can be used on an individual, small group, or class basis. In each lesson a narrator introduces the story, actors portray roles in the dramatization while music and other sound effects heighten pupil interest, reinforce reading skills, improve aural comprehension and oral reading, help diagnose a pupil's ability to comprehend ideas, and demonstrate correct pronunciation and intonation. This is especially good for bilingual students.

13. *Flash-X Material*　　　　　Educational Developmental
　　　　　　　　　　　　　　Laboratories, Inc.
　　　　　　　　　　　　　　1221 Avenue of The Americas
　　　　　　　　　　　　　　New York, New York 10020

Basic Sight Words
Sight Vocabulary Development

Intermediate-Senior High

This is a set of training materials for use with the EDL Flash-X apparatus or the individual hand tachistoscope. It is to be used for individual perceptual training, development of basic sight words and sight vocabulary development. There is a set of three levels of lessons 1-50.

14. *Goldman-Lynch Sounds*　　American Guidance Service, Inc.
　　and Symbols　　　　　　Department RT-L
　　Development Kit　　　　Circle Pines, Minnesota 55014
　　Phonetic Analysis

Primary-Intermediate-Junior High

This kit contains a puppet, tape cassettes, posters, picture cards, magnetic symbols and adventure story books. Sixty-four activities to stimulate production of the English speech sounds and recognition of their associated symbols.

15. *Junior-High Reading*　　　Coronet Instructional Media
　　Growth Series　　　　　65 E. South Water Street
　　　　　　　　　　　　　　Chicago, Illinois 60639

Basic Skills, Understanding Word Meanings, Getting the Big Ideas, Adjusting Reading Speed, Reading Creatively.

16. Language Master   Bell and Howell Company
                                     7100 McCormick Road
                                     Chicago, Illinois 60645
Vocabulary Development
Word Attack Skills (especially Structural
                    Analysis and Phonetic
                    Analysis)

   The Language Meter is a card reader. The student inserts a
card, watches, listens, records and then compares his responses
to the information on the instructor track. The programs include a phonics program, alphabet mastery program, vocabulary builder program, word-picture program, and a language
stimulation program. This program employs sight, speech,
touch, and hearing in coordinated, effective instruction. The
system includes a compact, portable unit which provides complete, self-contained dual track recording and playback capabil-
ity. The unit is used with sets of cards containing visual material
and a strip of magnetic recording tape.

17. New Advanced Reading   Reader's Digest Services Inc.
    Skill Builder   Educational Division
                                     Pleasantville, New York 10570
Comprehension Skills
Vocabulary Development
Study Skills

Intermediate-Adult

   This is a set of books with audio lesson units, advanced reading tutors at levels 7-8-9, and supplementary readers. It can be
used as a teacher's resource and audio aid. This program helps
to develop specific reading skills, such as recognizing main
ideas, noting sequence of events, etc. It is designed for use by
both good and reluctant readers to reinforce reading skills, improve aural comprehension, demonstrate correct pronunciation
and intonation, and serve as a model for class dramatization.

18. New Readers Press   Division of Laubach
                                     Literacy International 1980-1981
                                     Box 31
                                     Syracuse, New York 13210

Survival Reading

Intermediate-Adult

Books 2-8 progress in reading comprehension. Each book has 25 items of the subject pictured. Ten questions accompany each illustration, developing reading comprehension through three-level questioning system of fact finding, interpretation, and application. Answer keys are provided for self-correction.

Book 2: *Signs Around Town*
Book 3: *Label Talk*
Book 4: *Read the Instructions First*
Book 5: *Your Daily Paper*
Book 6: *It's on the Map*
Book 7: *Let's Look it Up*
Book 8: *Caution: Fine Print Ahead*

19. *Psychotechnics Radio*   Psychotechnics, Inc.
    Reading   1900 Pickwick Avenue
                                    Glenview, Illinois 60025

Vocabulary Development
Word Attack Skills
Comprehension Skills

Intermediate-Adult

This program contains thirty stories, fifteen tape cassettes, three hundred story booklets, two audio file cassette albums and a steel file cabinet. It is designed to attract reluctant readers and encourage the formation of good reading and listening habits. The program is useful in remedial training and in working with the culturally deprived.

20. *Vocabulary Audio*   Reader's Digest Service, Inc.
    Skills Lesson   Educational Division
                                    Pleasantville, New York 10570

Vocabulary Development
Word Attack Skills

Primary-Junior High

This program extends the audio program with dramatizations from thirty additional skill building stories. There are six vocabulary lessons on three cassettes at each level from 1-6. The program concentrates on developing word study or word analysis skills such as mastering words by matching words and definitions, using key words correctly, identifying words with sensory appeal, identifying the correct word, using context clues to identify meanings and using context clues to identify special meaning.

21. *Junior Scholastic*   Scholastic Book Services
                                 50 West 44 Street
                                 New York, New York 10036

Grades 6-8

Provides current affairs in an interesting way for children in grades 6-8. It is suggested for use in social studies, world history, U.S. history and world geography.

22. *Know Your World*   American Education Publications
                              Columbus, Ohio 43216

This eight page paper contains current events, articles, pictures and word and skill development exercises.

23. *Mainstream Books*   Charles E. Merrill Books, Inc.
                                1300 Alum Creek Drive
                                Columbus, Ohio 43216

Grades 4-7.5

Against the Odds
Courage Under Fire
They Were First
In New Directions
People Like You

Though geared to the inner-city student, these stories appeal to all students regardless of background or ability. Their dynamism lies in the diversity of problems that plague people—from those who are little known to well-known personalities.

24. *Open Door Series*   Children's Press
                                1224 W. VanBuren St.
                                Chicago, Illinois 60607

Grade 5

Autobiographies of special interest to minority group members. Includes guidance on career information in each author's career area.

25. *Read Magazine*   American Education Publications
                                   Columbus, Ohio 43216
    Grades 7-9

Through prose and poetry, *Read* aims at improving reading, writing, speaking, and listening skills.

26. *Bowmar Publishing*   622 Rodier Drive
    Corporation   Glendale, California 91201

    Drag Racing
    Slot Car Racing nad Motorcycle Racing
    Custom Cars
    Dune Buggies

Records, filmstrips and ten paperbacks for each title. For slow uninterested readers.

27. *Current Events*   Xerox Company
                                   Education Center
                                   Columbus, Ohio 43216
    Grades 7-8

This periodical features articles centered around daily news events that delve into geography, United States history, and civics.

28. *Gaining Independence in*   Charles E. Merrill Publishing Co.
    Reading Series   1300 Alum Creek Drive
                                   Columbus, Ohio 43216
    New Landmarks—Grade 4
    Bright Beacons—Grade 5

Short non-fictional reading selections, followed by exercises, lend themselves to specific skill work or as part of a developmental program.

29. *Target Books*   Garrard Publishing Company
                                      1607 North Market Street
                                      Champaign, Illinois 61820

    Grades 3-4

    Football Replay
    Women Who Dared to be Different
    Jazz Greats

    Each book individually planned to include several easy-to-read biographies abundantly illustrated with photographs tailored to the theme of the book.

30. *Teenage Tales*   D.C. Heath and Co.
                                      Division of Raytheon Ed. Co.
    Grades 7-12   2700 North Richard Avenue
                                      Indianapolis, Indiana 46219

31. *Scope*   Scholastic Book Services
                                      50 West 44 Street
                                      New York, New York 10036

    Grades 4-6

    Articles in this periodical cover contemporary topics of particular interest to teenagers. Included, are columns on films, music, family and teen problems. Puzzles, jokes, letters to the editor, and contest complete this well-rounded magazine.

32. *Urban World*   American Education Publications
                                      Columbus, Ohio 43216
    Grade 6

    Feature articles are centered around problems in the cities of today; shorter articles offer the serious and humorous side of topics of interest to teenagers.

APPENDIX B

Selected Commercial Tests for Reading Diagnosis

1. *Analytical Reading Inventory*   (Charles E. Merrill
                                      Publishing Co.)

Word recognition, oral accuracy, comprehension, functional level

Grades 1-9; 3 forms   Time: Varies

2. *Basic Reading Inventory*   (Kendall/Hunt
                                            Publishing Co.)

Word analysis, oral reading comprehension

Grades Preprimer-8   Time: Varies

3. *Classroom Reading Inventory*   (William C. Brown Co.)

Oral reading, comprehension, word recognition

Grades 2-8; 3 forms   Time: Varies

4. *Corrective Reading System*   (Psychotechnics, Inc.)

Word attack

Grades 1-6   Time: Varies

5. *Diagnostic Reading Scales*   (CTB/McGraw Hill, Inc.)

Oral reading, silent reading, word recognition, phonics

Grades 1-8   Time: 45 Min (Approx.)

6. *Durrell Analysis of Reading*   (Psychological
   Difficulty, 3rd Ed.   Corporation)

Oral and silent reading, listening comprehension and vocabulary, word recognition, spelling, visual memory, letter sounds, prereading phonics

Grades 1-6   Time: 30-90 Min.
                                            (Approx.)

7. *Gates-McKillop Reading*   (Teachers College Press)
   Diagnostic Tests

Oral reading, words and phrases flash, word recognition, knowledge of word parts, visual form of sounds, auditory blending, auditory discrimination, spelling, oral vocabulary, syllabication

Grades 1-6 (adult); 2 forms   Time: 45-90 Min.

8. *Gilmore Oral Reading Test*   (Psychological
                                          Corporation)

Oral reading rate and accuracy

Grades 1-8; 2 forms   Time: 15-25 Min.

9. *New Gray Oral Reading Test*   (Bobbs-Merrill Co.)

Oral reading grade level, comprehension estimate

Grades 1-adult; 4 forms   Time: 10-20 Min.

10. *Oral Reading Criterion Test*   (Dreier Educational
                                         Systems)

Oral reading, provides independent, instructional and frustrational reading levels

Grades 1-7   Time: Varies

11. *Reading Miscue Inventory*   (Macmillan Publishing
    (RMI)   Co.)

Phoneme/grapheme relationships, grammatical relationships, comprehension pattern, semantic similarity

Grades 1-7; tape recorder used   Time: Varies

12. *Reading Passages*   (CTB/McGraw-Hill)

Comprehension (determines independent, instructional and potential reading levels), rate

Grades 1-8; 2 forms   Time: 10-30 Min.

13. *Reading Placement Inventory*   (Brigham Young
                                         University Press)

Word recognition, oral reading, comprehension, functioning placement

Grades 1-9   Time: 30 Min.

14. *R/EAL Reading/Everyday*   (CAL Press, Inc.)
    Activities in Life

    Functional reading tasks

    Grades 1-5   Time: Varies

15. *Roswell-Chall Diagnostic*   (Essay Press)
    Reading Test of Word
    Analysis Skills

    Word recognition skills

    Grades 2-6; 2 forms   Time: 5 Min.

16. *Sipay Word-Analysis Tests*   (Educators Publishing
                                        Service, Inc.)

    Word-analysis skills (16 subtests)

    Grades 2-12   Time: Varies

17. *Slosson Oral Reading Test*   (Slosson Educational
                                        Publications)

    Estimates reading level through word pronunciation

    Grades 1-8

18. *Standard Reading Inventory*   (Klamath Printing Co.)

    Oral accuracy and level, silent reading and listening levels,
    word recognition

    Grades Preprimer-7; 2 forms   Time: 40-50 Min.

19. *Woodcock Reading Mastery*   (American Guidance
    Test   Service, Inc.)

    Sight vocabulary, letter identification, word and passage com-
    prehension, work attack

    Grades: K-12; 2 forms   Time: 20-30 Min.

GROUP TESTS FOR DIAGNOSIS

20. *Botel Reading Inventory*   (Follett Educational
                                       Corp.)

    Word recognition oral, word opposites, phonics mastery

    Grades 1-12; 2 forms   Time: 60 Min. (Approx.)

21. *California Phonics Survey*   (CTB/McGraw-Hill)
    Phonic analysis
    Grades 7-College   Time 45 Min.

22. *California Reading Test*   (CTB/McGraw-Hill)
    Vocabulary, comprehension
    Grades 4-14; 4 forms   Time: Varies

23. *Comprehension Tests of*   (CTB/McGraw-Hill)
    Basic Skills: Reading

    Vocabulary, comprehension
    Grades Level 2-4 to 6;   Time: Varies
    Level 3-6 to 8;
    Level 4-8 to 12

24. *Davis Reading Test*   (Psychological
                                       Corporation)

    Comprehension, rate

    Grades 8-11 & 11-13;   Time: 40 Min.
    4 forms each level

25. *Diagnostic Reading Tests*   (Committee on Diagnostic
    (diagnostic battery)   Reading Tests, Inc.)

    Lower Level Diagnosis: Vocabulary, silent and auditory com-
    prehension, rate, word attack

    Grades 4-8; 4 forms   Time Varies

    Upper Level Diagnosis: Vocabulary, comprehension, rate

    Grades 7-12; 4 forms   Time: Varies

26. *Doren Diagnostic Reading Test*   (American Guidance
   of Word Recognition Skills   Service)

 Letter and word recognition, comprehensive word attack skills

 Grades 1-9   Time: 1-3 Hours

27. *Durrell Listening-Reading*   (Psychological
   Series (Advanced)   Corporation)

 Vocabulary-listening and reading, comprehension-listening and reading

 Grades 7-9; 2 forms   Time: 80 Min.

28. *Gates-MacGinitie Reading*   (Teachers College Press)
   Tests

 Vocabulary, comprehension, speed

 Grades: Survey D—4-6; 3 forms   Time: 140-160 Min.
         Survey E—7-9; 3 forms
         Survey F—10-12; 2 forms

29. *High School Reading Test*   (Psychometric Affiliates)

 Vocabulary, word discrimination, sentence meaning, paragraph comprehension

 Grades 7-12; 2 forms   Time: 40 Min.

30. *Iowa Tests of Basic Skills*   (Houghton Mifflin)

 Vocabulary, comprehension, work-study skills

 Grades 3-8; 2 forms   Time: 67 Min.

31. *Iowa Tests of Educational*   (Science Research
   Development   Associates)

 Vocabulary, content area reading, using sources

 Grades 9-12   Time: Varies

32. *McCullough Word-Analysis*   (Personnel Press)
   Tests

Word attack skills

Grades 4-6   Time: 70 Min. (Approx.)

33. *McGraw-Hill Basic Skills*   (McGraw-Hill Book Co.)
    System: Reading

    Comprehension, skimming and scanning, rate and flexibility

    Grades 10-14; 2 forms   Time: 70 Min.

34. *Nelson-Denny Reading Test*   (Houghton Mifflin Co.)

    Vocabulary, comprehension, rate

    Grades 9-16; 2 forms   Time: 45-60 Min.

35. *New Developmental Reading*   (Lyons & Carnahan, Inc.)
    Tests (Intermediate Level)

    Vocabulary, reading for information, relationships, interpretation and appreciation

    Grades 3-7; 2 forms   Time: 75 Min.

36. *Silent Reading Diagnostic*   (Lyons & Carnahan, Inc.)
    Tests

    Word recognition, structural analysis, phonic analysis

    Grades 3-8   Time: 90 Min.

37. *Stanford Diagnostic Reading*   (Harcourt Brace
    Tests   Jovanovich, Inc.)

    Green Level Diagnosis: Auditory vocabulary, auditory discrimination, phonetic analysis, structural analysis, reading comprehension

    Grades 3-5; 2 forms   Time: 75 Min.

    Brown Level Diagnosis: Phonetic and structural analysis, vocabulary, comprehension, rate

    Grades 5-8; 2 forms   Time: 93 Timed Min.

    Blue Level Diagnosis: Phonetic and structural analysis, vocabulary, comprehension, rate, scanning and skimming

Grades 9-12; 2 forms   Time: 96 Timed Min.

38. *The Traxler High School*   (Bobbs-Merrill Company,
    Reading Test   Inc.)

Reading rate, story comprehension, main ideas, total comprehension

Grades 10-12; 2 forms   Time: 60 Min.

39. *The Traxler Silent Reading*   (Bobbs-Merrill Company,
    Test   Inc.)

Comprehension, rate, vocabulary

Grades: 7-10; 4 forms   Time: 46 Timed Min.

40. *Watson-Glaser Critical*   (Harcourt Brace
    Thinking Appraisal   Jovanovich, Inc.)

Inference, recognizing assumptions, interpretation, deduction, evaluation of arguments

Grades 9-16   Time: 60 Min.

APPENDIX C

Annotated Professional Book List for Teachers

1. Alexander, Jr. Estill *et al.* Teaching Reading. Boston: Little, Brown and Company, 1970.

   This text covers all the components of the reading process from reading readiness to the development of study skills and classroom organization.

2. Aulls, Mark W. *Developmental and Remedial Reading in the Middle Grades* (abridged). Boston: Allyn and Bacon, Inc., 1978.

   This guide to teaching middle school students contains materials on acquiring textbook reading skills and developing writing abilities.

3. Bader, Lois, A. *Reading Diagnosis and Remediation in Class-room and Clinic.* New York: Macmillan Publishing Co., Co., Inc., 1980.

Bader's treatment of the assessment and correction of reading deficiencies places a great deal of importance on the integration of diagnosis and remediation with special emphasis on comprehension difficulties. Case studies and examples of diagnostic tests are included.

4. Bond, Guy L., Miles A. Tinker, and Barbara B. Wasson. *Reading Difficulties—Their Diagnosis and Correction* (4th Ed.). Englewood Cliffs, N.J.: Prentice-Hall, Inc., 1979.

The major purpose of this important volume is that of providing information relative to the treatment of special problems of disabled readers and the selection of teaching methods for the handicapped reader. Case studies and suggestions for further readings are included.

5. Burmeister, Lou E. *Reading Strategies for Middle and Secondary School Teachers* (2nd Ed.). Reading, Massachusetts: Addison-Wesley Publishing Company, 1978.

Burmeister discusses the process of adjusting reading instruction to meet the individual needs of middle and secondary school students.

6. Burns, Paul C. and Betty D. Roe. *Informal Reading Assessment.* Chicago: Rand McNally College Publishing Company, 1980.

This manual provides graded word lists and passages for use in informal reading assessment for readers from the pre-primer level through the twelfth grade.

7. Burns, Paul C. and Betty D. Roe. *Reading Activities for Today's Elementary Schools.* Chicago: Rand McNally College Publishing Company, 1979.

Burns and Roe report on suggested pre-reading experiences, the development of word recognition, the enlargement of vocabulary and comprehension, and offer ideas on improving content area reading for primary and intermediate students.

8. Burns, Paul C. and Betty D. Roe. *Teaching Reading in Today's Elementary Schools* (2nd Ed.). Chicago: Rand McNally College Publishing Company, 1980.

This important volume contains a discussion relative to the development of the reading act and covers a range of topics from reading readiness to study skills and classroom management. A special section is devoted to elementary readers with special needs.

9. Bush, Clifford L. and Mildred H. Heubner. *Strategies for Reading in The Elementary School* (2nd Ed.). New York: Macmillan Publishing Co., Inc., 1979.

The structure and content of effective reading programs are described in this important professional book for teachers.

10. Carnine, Douglas and Jerry Silbert. *Direct Instruction Reading*. Columbus: Charles E. Merrill Publishing Company, 1979.

Carnine and Silbert focus on strategies for teaching basic reading skills to students with special needs and include instructional alternatives for cases when the primary techniques fail. The appendices contain word lists, bibliographies for student reading, and lesson outlines.

11. Carrillo, Lawrence. W. *Teaching Reading: A Handbook*. New York: St. Martin's Press, 1976.

This handbook for teachers outlines approaches to reading instruction, describes factors related to reading difficulties, and analyzes the characteristics of successful remedial programs.

12. Cheek, Martha Collins and Earl H. Cheek Jr. *Diagnostic-Prescriptive Reading Instruction*. Dubuque, Iowa: Wm. C. Brown Company Publishers, 1980.

The development of a diagnostic-prescriptive reading program for elementary and middle school students is described.

Suggestions for diagnostic procedures and classroom organization are included.

13. Cooper, J. David et al. *The What and How of Reading Instruction*. Columbus: Charles E. Merrill Publishing Company, 1979.

   This examination of reading instruction presents six modules which lead both preservice and in-service teachers through basic teaching strategies. The modules cover comprehension, word recognition, study skills, directed teaching strategies, assessment of reading levels and skills, and classroom organization and management.

14. Cushenbery, Donald C. *Reading Improvement Through Diagnosis, Remediation and Individualized Instruction*. West Nyack, New York: Parker Publishing Company, 1977.

   This volume contains important information on such topics as motivation, developmental reading programs, developing word recognition and comprehension skills, and effective diagnostic and remedial strategies.

15. Dechant, Emerald V. and Henry P. Smith. *Psychology in Teaching Reading*. Englewood Cliffs, N.J.: Prentice-Hall, Inc., 1977.

   Dechant and Smith examine psychological factors which influence reading behaviors. Their volume covers psychological bases of readiness, interest, and personality factors in the reading process as well as other facets of the reading process which involve psychological components.

16. Dillner, Martha H. and Joanne P. Olson. *Personalizing Reading Instruction in Middle, Junior, and Senior High Schools*. New York: Macmillan Publishing Co., Inc., 1977.

   Diagnostic-prescriptive instruction forms the basis of the program of individualized reading instruction ascribed in this work. The effective use of materials is also included.

17. Duffy, Gerald G. and George B. Sherman. *Systematic Reading*

Instruction (2nd Ed.). New York: Harper & Row, Publishers, 1977.

Duffy and Sherman have designed a series of skill modules for the systematic development of basic reading skills. The appendices contain diagnostic charts, skill objectives, and a bibliography of practice materials for the student.

18. Durkin, Dolores. *Teaching Young Children to Read* (2nd Ed.). Boston: Allyn and Bacon, Inc., 1976.

This instructional guide for teachers of young readers examines reading readiness and the various components of reading competency. Durkin also provides a series of sample lessons for the teacher's use.

19. Ekwall, Eldon, E. *Diagnosis and Remediation of the Disabled Reader*. Boston: Allyn and Bacon, Inc., 1976.

After discussing the causes of reading failure, Ekwall offers suggestions for the diagnosis and remediation of reading difficulties. Reading tests and inventories, as well as suggested materials for reading skill development, are included in the appendices.

20. Ekwall, Eldon E. *Locating and Correcting Reading Disabilities* (2nd Ed.). Columbus: Charles E. Merrill Publishing Company, 1977.

The role of reading difficulties is discussed. Many techniques relating to the correction of reading difficulties are described.

21. Estes, Thomas A. and Joseph L. Vaughn, Jr. *Reading and Learning in the Content Classroom* (abridged). Boston: Allyn and Bacon, Inc., 1978.

Estes and Vaughn outline ways of utilizing lessons for the development of reading skills.

22. Fry, Edward B. *Elementary Reading Instruction*. New York: McGraw-Hill Book Company, 1977.

Dr. Fry provides an in-depth discussion of several pertinent topics including reading readiness, methods of teaching reading, and evaluation and grouping.

23. Gibson, Eleanor J. and Harry Levin. *The Psychology of Reading*. Cambridge, Massachusetts: The MIT Press, 1976.

Gibson and Levin provide an analysis of the psychological components of the reading process.

24. Gillespie-Silver, Patricia. *Teaching Reading to Children with Special Needs*. Columbus: Charles E. Merrill Publishing Company, 1979.

The assessment process and methods of instruction for students with special needs are discussed in this important professional work.

25. Guszak, Frank J. *Diagnostic Reading Instruction in the Elementary School* (2nd Ed.). New York: Harper & Row, Publishers, 1978.

Guszak describes many valuable strategies for undertaking diagnostic reading instruction in the elementary school.

26. Hafner, Lawrence E. *Developmental Reading in Middle and Secondary Schools: Foundations, Strategies, and Skills for Teaching*. New York: Macmillan Publishing Co., Inc., 1977.

This guide to reading instruction focuses on strategies for further development of the skills for readers in middle and secondary schools.

27. Harris, Albert J. and Edward R. Sipay. *How to Teach Reading*. New York: Longman, Inc., 1979.

This treatment of reading instruction in the elementary school provides modules for competency-based learning and includes ideas for helping students who have special needs.

28. Heilman, Arthur W. *Principles and Practices of Teaching Reading* (4th Ed.). Columbus: Charles E. Merrill Publishing Company, 1977.

Several important aspects of the reading process are considered in this book. Heilman also discusses reading readiness, activities for beginning readers, classroom organization, and the culturally different students.

29. Herber, Harold L. *Teaching Reading in Content Areas* (2nd Ed.). Englewood Cliffs, N.J.: Prentice-Hall, Inc., 1978.

Herber discusses the need for and methods of extending reading instruction to content area classrooms. The appendices contain sample instructional materials.

30. Hill, Walter R. *Secondary School Reading: Process, Program, Procedure.* Boston: Allyn and Bacon, Inc., 1979.

This examination of reading instruction for secondary students aims at developing a comprehensive program to ensure competencies. The appendices contain extensive listings of upper grade reading assessment materials and bibliographies of appropriate sources for secondary readers.

31. Hittleman, Daniel R. *Developmental Reading: A Psycholinguistic Perspective.* Chicago: Rand McNally College Publishing Company, 1978.

This text is aimed at teachers in training. Hittleman discusses strategies for reading development and offers suggestions for work with students with special needs.

32. Ives, Josephine P., Laura Z. Bursuk, and Sumner A. Ives. *Word Identification Techniques.* Chicago: Rand McNally College Publishing Company, 1979.

Word identification is described as the basis of all other reading skills. This volume contains extensive discussions of the many word identification techniques available for the busy teacher.

33. Johnson, Dale D. and P. David Pearson. *Teaching Reading Vocabulary.* New York: Holt, Rinehart, and Winston, 1978.

Johnson and Pearson provide a discussion of the development of basic sight and meaning vocabularies and of the use of various techniques for enlargement of total vocabulary.

34. Kaluger, George and Clifford J. Kolson. *Reading and Learning Disabilities* (2nd Ed.). Columbus: Charles E. Merrill Publishing Company, 1978.

The authors contend that educators must provide individualized remedial help for readers with difficulties. Special attention is given to the problems of learning disabled students.

35. Kennedy, Eddie C. *Classroom Approaches to Remedial Reading* (2nd Ed.). Itasca, Illinois: F. E. Peacock Publishers, Inc., 1977.

Methods of diagnosis and remediation are discussed in this important treatment of reading difficulties. Special attention is given to the needs of disadvantaged students and slow learners.

36. Kirk, Samuel A., Sister Joanne Marie Kleibhan, and Janet W. Lerner. *Teaching Reading to Slow and Disabled Learners*. Boston: Houghton Mifflin Company, 1978.

Kirk, Kleibhan and Lerner investigate ways of adjusting reading instruction to the needs of different learners. Their analysis includes specialized remedial reading techniques and discussion of research relating to slow and disabled students.

37. Kochevar, Deloise E. *Individualized Remedial Reading Techniques for the Classroom Teacher*. West Nyack, New York: Parker Publishing Company, Inc., 1975.

Kochevar describes how to develop an individualized classroom remediation program for the teacher who lacks special facilities.

38. Lapp, Diane and James Flood. *Teaching Reading to Every Child*. New York: Macmillan Publishing Co., Inc., 1978.

This guide to the teaching of reading covers reading readiness, word analysis and comprehension, the development of study skills, and the special needs of bilingual students.

34. Mangrum, Charles T. III, and Harry W. Forgan. *Developing Competencies in Teaching Reading*. Columbus: Charles E. Merrill Publishing Company, 1979.

Mangrum and Forgan have designed a modular format to help teachers of elementary or middle schools develop 13 basic competencies in reading instruction.

40. McNeil, John D., Lisbeth Donant, and Marvin C. Alkin. *How to Teach Reading Successfully*. Boston: Little, Brown and Company, 1980.

This reading guide focuses on elementary teachers and the range of approaches to the teaching task that are available. A section on meeting special needs is included.

41. Murray, Frank B. and John J. Pikulski. *The Acquisition of Reading: Cognitive, Linguistic, and Perceptual Prerequisites*. Baltimore: University Park Press, 1978.

This collection of essays by reading authorities focuses on various prerequisites to the development of reading skills.

42. Quandt, Ivan J. *Teaching Reading: A Human Process*. Chicago: Rand McNally College Publishing Company, 1977.

Quandt evaluates the various components of the reading process and discusses the language-experience, individualized book, basal skills-oriented, and thematic approaches to instruction.

43. *Reading Horizons: Selected Readings*. Edited by Kenneth VenderMeulen. Kalamazoo, Michigan: Western Michigan University Press, 1979.

This collection of essays by reading authorities offers a range of views on the professional preparation of teachers, tests and inventories, administrators and reading programs, and strategies for instruction.

44. Robinson, H. Alan. *Teaching Reading and Study Strategies: The Content Areas* (2nd Ed.). Boston: Allyn and Bacon, Inc., 1978.

These methods of reading instruction are aimed at secondary school teachers. Special emphasis is placed on the development and use of reading skills in other content area classrooms.

45. Roe, Betty D., Barbara D. Stoodt, and Paul C. Burns. *Reading Instruction in the Secondary School*. Chicago: Rand McNally College Publishing Company, 1978.

    Roe, Stoodt, and Burns combine a thorough discussion of the reading process with practical suggestions for building secondary school reading programs.

46. Rupley, William H., and Timothy R. Blair. *Reading Diagnosis and Remediation: A Primer for Classroom and Clinic*. Chicago: Rand McNally College Publishing Company, 1979.

    The diagnostic model of instruction is the core of this examination of reading programs. Rupley and Blair include case studies and guidelines for the selection and interpretation of diagnostic tests, as well as corrective techniques for use in the classroom and clinic.

47. Salvia, John and James E. Ysseldyke. *Assessment in Special and Remedial Education*. Boston: Houghton Mifflin Company, 1978.

    This guide to assessment in special and remedial education contains extensive information on the purposes, assumptions, reliability, and applications of assessment devices.

48. Savage, John F. and Jean F. Mooney. *Teaching Reading to Children with Special Needs*. Boston: Allyn and Bacon, Inc., 1979.

    Savage and Mooney discuss learning disorders and physical and emotional problems. They offer information on organizing a program for children with special needs within the regular classroom.

49. Schell, Leo M. *Fundamentals of Decoding for Teachers* (2nd Ed.). Chicago: Rand McNally College Publishing Company, 1979.

This handbook provides instruction in the principles of "decoding" (phonic and structural analysis) for teachers and student teachers.

50. Shepherd, David L. *Comprehensive High School Reading Methods* (2nd Ed.). Columbus: Charles E. Merrill Publishing Company, 1978.

The comprehensive high school reading program is described as one in which the reading skills which are developed are consciously applied to the classes in other content areas.

51. Singer, Harry and Dan Donlan. *Reading and Learning from Text*. Boston: Little, Brown and Company, 1980.

Singer and Donlan discuss strategies for teaching reading to students with a wide range of abilities. Special emphasis is given to the teaching-learning processes at the secondary level.

52. Smith, Richard J. And Dale D. Johnson. *Teaching Children to Read*. Reading, Massachusetts: Addison-Wesley Publishing Company, 1976.

This discussion of reading instruction includes information on the selection of reading materials and offers various approaches to the task of remediation.

53. Smith, Richard J., Wayne Ottot, and Lee Hansen. *The School Reading Program*. Boston: Houghton Mifflin Company, 1978.

Reading teachers, supervisors, and specialists will be particularly interested in this handbook. Pertinent information is provided regarding the formation and administration of reading programs.

54. Spache, George D. *Diagnosing and Correcting Reading Disabilities*. Boston: Allyn and Bacon, Inc., 1976.

Dr. Spache provides a thorough discussion of the proper administration and interpretation of various diagnostic techniques and offers a number of strategies for the remediation of reading deficiencies.

55. Stauffer, Russell G., Jules C. Abrams, and John J. Pikulski. *Diagnosis, Correction, and Prevention of Reading Disabilities.* New York: Harper & Row, Publishers, 1978.

   The prevention of reading problems through the use of assessment tools is discussed. Diagnosis and remediation of reading disabilities is the major theme of the volume.

56. Tierney, Robert J., John E. Readence, and Ernest K. Dishner. *Reading Strategies and Practices: A Guide for Improving Instruction.* Boston: Allyn and Bacon, Inc., 1980.

   Among the strategies and practices contained in this volume are methods for improving comprehension, content area reading, and study skills. The authors also suggest ways of appraising teacher effectiveness and include extensive appendices with ideas for student activities.

57. Veatch, Jeanette et al. *Key Words to Reading.* Columbus: Charles E. Merrill Publishing Company, 1979.

   This approach to the reading process is based on the acquisition of a key vocabulary.

58. Weimer, Wayne, and Ann Weimer. *Reading Readiness Inventory.* Columbus: Charles E. Merrill Publishing Company, 1977.

   The Reading Readiness Inventory tests perceptual, sensory, and mental development. It can be administered either individually or in a group and includes subtests on visual motor activity, auditory discrimination, verbalization, and word recognition and reproduction as well as suggestions for readiness activities.

59. Wilson, Robert M. *Diagnostic and Remedial Reading for Classroom and Clinic* (3rd Ed.). Columbus: Charles E. Merrill Publishing Company, 1977.

   Dealing with problem readers is the major subject of this volume. Wilson gives extensive suggestions for remedial activities and also discusses the respective roles of parents and professionals.

60. Zintz, Miles V. *Corrective Reading* (3rd Ed.). Dubuque, Iowa: Wm. C. Brown Company, 1977.

This analysis of corrective reading instruction offers suggestions for using the development of writing skills to enhance acquisition of reading competencies. Zintz also provides a bibliography of books for corrective reading.

APPENDIX D

List of Publishers of Educational Materials

Allyn and Bacon, Inc.
470 Atlantic Avenue
Boston, Massachusetts 02210

American Education
Publications
Columbus, Ohio 43216

American Guidance Service,
Inc.
Department RT-L
Circle Pines, Minnesota 55014

Barnell-Loft Ltd.
958 Church Street
Baldwin, New York 11510

Bell and Howell Company
7100 McCormick Road
Chicago, Illinois 60645

The Bobbs-Merrill Co., Inc.
4300 West 62nd Street
Indianapolis, Indiana 46268

Bowmer Publishing Corporation
622 Rodier Drive
Glendale, California 91201

Brigham Young University
Press
205 University Press Building
Provo, Utah 84602

California Test Bureau
5916 Hollywood Boulevard
Los Angeles, California 90029

California Press, Inc.
76 Madison Avenue
New York, New York 10016

(The) Center for Applied
Research in Education
Box 130
West Nyack, New York 10995

Charles E. Merrill Publishing
Company
1300 Alum Creek Drive
Columbus, Ohio 43216

Children's Press
1224 West Van Buren Street
Chicago, Illinois 60607

Committee on Diagnostic
Reading Tests, Inc.
Mountain Home, North Carolina
28758

Computerland
14400 Catalina Street
San Leandro, California 94577

Computerland
Rockbrook Village
108th and Center
Omaha, Nebraska 68144

Control Data Corporate
Headquarters
P. O. Box 0
Minneapolis, Minnesota 55440

Coronet Instructional Media
65 East South Water Street
Chicago, Ilinois 60639

CTB/McGraw-Hill
Del Monte Research Park
Monterey, California 93940

Developmental Learning
Materials
7440 Natchez Avenue
Niles, Illinois 50548

Drein Educational Systems
320 Raritan Avenue
Highland Park, New Jersey
08904

Educational Development
Laboratories, Inc.
(Division of McGraw-Hill, Inc.)

Educational Progress
Corporation
P. O. Box 45663
Tulsa, Oklahoma 74145

Educators Publishing Service
75 Moulton Street
Cambridge, Massachusetts
02138

Essay Press
Box 5
Planetarium Station
New York, New York 10024

Follett Educational Corporation
1010 West Washington
Boulevard
Chicago, Illinois 60607

Garrard Publishing Company
107 Cherry Street
New Canaan, Conn. 06840

Harcourt Brace Jovanovich, Inc.
757 Third Avenue
New York, New York 10017

(D. C.) Heath and Company
Division of Raytheon Ed.
Company
2700 North Richard Avenue
Indianapolis, Indiana 46219

Holt, Rinehart & Winston, Inc.
383 Madison Avenue
New York, New York 10017

Houghton Mifflin Company
110 Fremont Street
Boston, Massachusetts 02107

Ideal School Supply
Oak Lawn, Illinois 60453

Imperial International Learning
Corporation
P. O. Box 548
Kankakee, Illinois 60901

Kendall/Hunt Publishing
Company
2460 Kerper Boulevard
Dubuque, Iowa 52001

Kenworthy Educational
Service, Inc.
138 Allen Street
Buffalo, New York 14205

Keystone View Company
Meadville, Pennsylvania 16335

King Features
Department 1344
235 East 45th Street
New York, New York 10017

Klamath Printing Company
Klamath, Oregon 97601

Lyons & Carnahan, Publishers
407 East 25th Street
Chicago, Illinois 60616

Macmillan Publishing Co., Inc.
60 Fifth Avenue
New York, New York 10011

McGraw-Hill Book Company
1221 Avenue of the Americas
New York, New York 10036

New Readers Press
Division of Laubach Literacy
International
Box 31
Syracuse, New York 13210

Parker Publishing Company,
Inc.
West Nyack, New York 10994

Personnel Press
191 Spring Street
Lexington, Massachusetts 02173

Prentice-Hall, Inc.
Educational Book Division
Englewood Cliffs, New Jersey
07632

The Psychological Corporation
757 Third Avenue
New York, New York 10017

Psychotechnics, Inc.
1900 Pickwick Avenue
Glenview, Illinois 60025

Radio Shack Computer Center
3006 Dodge
Omaha, Nebraska 68131

Rand McNally
P. O. Box 7600
Chicago, Illinois 60680

Readers Digest Services, Inc.
Educational Division
Pleasantville, New York 10570

Scholastic Book Services
50 West 44 Street
New York, New York 10036

Science Research Associates
259 East Erie Street
Chicago, Illinois 60611

Slosson Educational
Publications
140 Pine Street
East Aurora, New York 14052

Teachers College Press
Teachers College, Columbia
University
525 West 120th Street
New York, New York

Teaching Resources
Corporation
50 Pond Park Boulevard
Hingham, Massachusetts 02043

Xerox Education Publications
Education Center
Columbus, Ohio 43216

Index